MW01062929

FOR GOD'S GLORY

NEW LIFE BOUGHT WITH THE BLOOD OF CHRIST

REPENT...BELIEVE...RECEIVE

CHERYL D. BRADY

Xulon PRESS

FOREWORD

Forty years of wandering in darkness. Sound familiar? All the riches a man of the world could desire yet still have emptiness. God did not tell me or ask me to change my heart, but because with Him all things are possible, His mercy and love opened my eyes and ears to His Word and left the choice up to me. There are those secured by His grace in His fold whom He uses as vessels of His Word each and every day. Cheryl Brady is one of those chosen by God to cross the paths of many on their life's journey, to sow His seeds, to reap His harvest, to gather His flock, and to rally His troops.

Her words are His words directly from the Source of all things—God. We all must question whose camp we are in and come to terms with our relationship with God and His Son, Jesus Christ. I have had the privilege of previewing many of the questions in this book over the last two years. One must think about and account for his present position in life. It will make both believer and non-believer recognize with humility or arrogance where they stand.

I am unworthy of any gift from God, but by His grace He has blessed me and countless others with such a gift as Cheryl. Her efforts in *For God's Glory* are for the glory of

God. As you finish this book, recognize that we are on notice and can no longer deny the issues of our salvation that are at hand. Take to heart what is written and make the move, for only God knows what is in a man's heart.

Al Starostanko

TABLE OF CONTENTS

INTRODUCTION.. ix

CHAPTER 1
    Your Life Is No Longer Your Own 15

CHAPTER 2
    Get Out of the Enemy's Camp.............................21

CHAPTER 3
    Pretending Submission to God.............................35

CHAPTER 4
    The Road to Salvation...49

CHAPTER 5
    Where Are the Laborers? 71

CHAPTER 6
    Spiritual Check-up: How's Your Walk
    by Faith?..89

CHAPTER 7
    GOD – The Sovereign LORD of Heaven
    and Earth 111

INTRODUCTION

I did not choose God; God chose me. The Bible says that the sheep hear the Shepherd's voice. God called out to me, and I responded to the call. I can do nothing on my own. It is by God's grace that the word came to me on several occasions to write this book. It is also quite interesting how a series of articles and papers on Christian living that were written to encourage my brothers and sisters in Christ and as a means to try and turn some from sin have now all come together to form the chapters of this book. It is God who works in us both to will and to do for His good pleasure. I did not choose this important topic of obedience, but rather it came by inspiration from God. The message that God is sending is clear: Obey Him and live...repent (turn from sin to God)...believe (put your trust in Jesus by keeping His Word)...receive (life from the Holy Spirit, the guarantee of your eternal inheritance).

My profession: career officer, United States Army. My calling: to serve as ambassador for my King, the Lord Jesus Christ. Both come at a great cost. Both are a call to sacrifice and obedience. Both are a means, an instrument, through which a man, by God's grace and mercy, may be saved and set free. Both are a means to bring about peace. One brings peace in the physical world in the life of man, and the other in the spiritual world in the unseen heart of man. One operates in the natural realm with manmade weapon systems to deliver those who are oppressed and suffer at the hands of evil and ungodly men, while the other operates in the spiritual realm with words of reconciliation and hope, words of salvation to deliver, to set the captives free from sin. "How beautiful upon the mountains are the feet of him who brings good news, who proclaims peace, who brings glad tidings of good things, who proclaims salvation" (Isaiah 52:7).

In order to gain peace and freedom—for those who are oppressed and held captive (in the natural by man and in the spiritual by sin and Satan) to be released—someone oftentimes has to die (lose his life) so that others may live. The freedom that man brings is temporary. The freedom that comes *For God's Glory* with the new life bought with the blood of Christ—the freedom that Christ gives—is eternal, forever.

Jesus gave His life so that the world through faith in Him may live (John 3:16-17). God was in Christ reconciling the world to Himself, and He purchased the church with His own blood (1 Corinthians 5:19; Acts 20:28). The mission assigned to Jesus—the work He came to do—was a monumental task, one that no mere man could accomplish. The eternal consequences for all mankind rested upon His shoulders. He had to live by every word that proceeded from the mouth of His Father. There was no margin for error, no room for disobedience. The slightest hint of doubt in what the Father promised His Son, I believe, would have spelled disaster for all mankind. If Jesus had doubted any of the words that He received from the Father, He may have disobeyed (fallen short of God's glory). Had Jesus disobeyed, none of the human race would be made righteous (Romans 5:19). Had Jesus disobeyed, His sacrifice would have been unacceptable to God because it would have had a spot, a blemish.

And, lastly, had it been unacceptable, the Father never would have raised Jesus His Son from the grave to life. He never would have given Jesus the power to give life. As a result, we would all be without hope for a better life, without any hope of ever being reconciled to God or being justified in order that we might obtain eternal life.

Nevertheless, the Father encouraged the Son, for He said of Jesus, "This is My beloved Son in whom I am well pleased" (Matthew 3:17). And we know that Jesus had the victory over sin, for it is written in John 19:28 that after this, Jesus, knowing that all things were now accomplished that the Scripture might be fulfilled, said, "I thirst." On that old rugged cross on Cavalry before He bowed His head and gave up His spirit, He said, "It is finished!"

"Therefore I say to you, her sins, which are many, are forgiven, for she loved much. But to whom little is forgiven, the same loves little" (Luke 7:47). **A Christian's gratitude changes his attitude, which in turn increases his altitude.** If we are truly grateful for what Christ suffered and endured on our behalf—the horrible death for our many sins and His forgiveness of those sins—then our gratitude would change our attitude toward sin and obedience to God, and that change would lead to an increase in our altitude (our intimacy and closeness with our heavenly Father).

Our love for God as evidenced by our obedience to His Word and the visibility of our actions as Christians toward Him comes from the realization of the depth of our sins. If, in our eyes, our sins are little that Christ has forgiven, then we will love little. If, on the other hand, we see our sins as many, we will love much. It is our love for Jesus Christ that demonstrates our true faith in God.

All Christians will not love God the same because all will not equally appreciate the magnitude of God's mercy in saving them from eternal death. **God wants us to love Him by obeying (hearing) His Son and His Word. And**

because we obey, we show the evidence, the visible proof, of our trust in Christ.

This obedience, as seen by others on the outside, comes as a result of the work being done by the Holy Spirit on the inside. God wants us to draw near to Him by obeying the first and greatest commandment, which is to love our God with all of our heart, mind, and soul, and the second, which is like it, to love our neighbor as ourselves. **In our love for God through obedience, God's love can be poured out into the world.**

Jesus did not die on the cross for His own sins, for He had none. He died for the sins of the whole human race—people from every nation and every tongue. Hear what the Word of God says about Jesus:

> He gave His back to those who struck Him, and His cheeks to those who plucked out the beard. He did not hide His face from shame and spitting.

> He was wounded for our transgressions. He was bruised for our iniquities. The chastisement for our peace was upon Him, and by His stripes we are healed. We have turned, every one, to his own way, and the LORD has laid on Him the iniquity of us all. He was oppressed and He was afflicted, yet He opened not His mouth. He was led as a lamb to the slaughter, and as a sheep before its shearers is silent, so He opened not His mouth. He was taken from prison and from judgment. They pierced His hands and His feet. They divided His garments among them, and for His clothing they cast lots. He was cut off from the land of the living. For the transgression of

His people He was stricken. They made His
grave with the wicked, but with the rich at
His death, because He had done no violence,
nor was any deceit in His mouth.

Isaiah 50:6; 53:5-9

Jesus died to set all mankind free from slavery and
bondage to sin. All who believe this will have new life,
eternal life. Jesus' death on the cross is difficult for mankind
to understand. God tells us simply to believe in order to be
saved. He never tells us to understand in order to be saved.
We can believe without understanding. But we will never
understand until we believe. Faith that pleases God is to
believe because He said it.

Now is the time for true Christians to start living as
though they believe what the Bible says, as though they
believe what Jesus taught. Christians must stand firm on
God's Word and stop wavering and doubting God. We must
prove our commitment to Jesus by the life we live. **How a
Christian lives his life each day (either in obedience or
disobedience, submission or rebellion) will show whether
or not he is truly grateful and thankful for Jesus' sacrifice for his sins.** He will love much if he recognizes that he
has been forgiven much. His life will show if he is a good
tree producing good fruit or a bad tree producing bad fruit.
A Christian's lifestyle, which flows from his love for God,
will show evidence to all who witness it that he has new life
bought with the blood of Christ.

CHAPTER 1

YOUR LIFE IS NO LONGER YOUR OWN

> You are witnesses against yourselves that you
> have chosen the Lord for yourselves, to serve
> Him (Joshua 24:22).

This was Joshua's reply to the people of Israel after they told him that they were determined to serve the Lord. When Joshua told the Israelites to choose for themselves whom they would serve, he was telling them to choose life by obeying the laws of God and keeping God's statutes and His commandments, by keeping the covenant. Or they could choose death by continuing to follow the false gods, by continuing in idolatry. To follow and obey any other teaching than what is written in the Bible is false worship. It is evil. It is sin because it leads a person away from the true and living God.

The people acknowledged that they were accountable for their decision. Christians are just as accountable today as the people of Israel were back then for their decision to serve and follow Christ. When a sinner saved by grace through faith in Christ says yes to God, he should know what he is committing himself to. He must count the costs. Life is no longer about him. It is about Christ and it is about the things of God. It is no longer the believer who lives, but Christ who lives in him.

He came to Christ for salvation. He said yes to God. Yes, I will obey Your Word and Your commandments. I will do what You tell me to do. At that moment he gave up all rights to himself; his life is no longer his own to live how he pleases. But in reality some have lived each day as if their life still belonged to them. They have lied to God.

With their mouths they said yes to God, but their hearts are far from Him. Their lifestyle is witness against them that Jesus Christ is not Lord of their life. They continue doing what they want to do, how they want to do it, without any regard for what the Word of God says concerning how they are to live as a child of God. They have not put off the old man—crucified the flesh—so therefore they do not live as a new creature in Christ. Friendship with the world is enmity with God. Those who want friendship with the world make themselves an enemy of God (James 4:4). Be doers of the Word, and not hearers only, deceiving yourselves (James 1:22). You can continue traveling the broad road that leads to destruction **thinking** you are on the narrow path of everlasting life or you can **know for sure.** The problem with thinking you are saved versus knowing by belief in Christ is that the mind changes like the wind. A believing heart is set on God and the things of God. Once it has been changed by God (circumcised by Him), it remains loyal to Him. The children—true children—of God do those things that please their heavenly Father. The evidence as to whom they serve (God or Satan) is in their lifestyle and obedience as the two line up with the Scriptures. You may have heard the old saying, "Who's fooling whom?"

The Lord knows those who are his...Those
who claim they belong to the Lord must turn
away from **all** wickedness.
2 Timothy 2:19 NLT (emphasis added)

Nothing a man says, thinks, or does escapes the eyes and
ears of the Holy One, the all-knowing God. (See Psalm 139
concerning God's perfect knowledge of man.)

All things lay naked before Him. We will one day
give an account of what we have done in this earthly body
(Ecclesiastes 12:13-14; 2 Corinthians 5:10). A sinful lifestyle
gives the enemies of the Lord great opportunity to despise
and blaspheme (2 Samuel 12:14; Romans 2:24).

Stop for a moment and take inventory of your life. Take
a look at what you've done day in and day out, week after
week, month after month, year after year since you came
to Christ for your salvation. Are you a Christian in name
only? You must both walk the walk and live the talk, or step
away from using the name of the Lord in vain, for it is sin.
God commands that we not take the name of the Lord our
God in vain.

If you say you are a Christian, then live as though you
really are. As a Christian you represent Christ at all times. Do
you love God? If yes, then obey His commandments. Live
as a child of God who is in this world but not of this world.
Stop doing the things that a child of God ought not do. The
time has come to stop playing foolish and childish games
with God. Now that you are an adult, you should put away
childish things. Some have been claiming to be a Christian
far too long to continue living the way they do. If they really
knew God and how His anger burns against them because of
their disobedience/rebellion—how He grieves because they
play the harlot with the world and the things of the world.
If they really knew God, they would stop and come to Him,
repent and ask forgiveness for their sins—loving Him as

17

He deserves to be loved, serving, praising, and worshipping Him as only He deserves.

The power, justice, and righteousness of almighty God is not something to take lightly or for granted. God is a God to be reckoned with, not to play or contend with. Do you not know what He did to Lucifer and the angels who rebelled against Him in heaven? Do you not know that He opened closed wombs for women to bring forth life? Do you not know what He did in Egypt—how He visited every Egyptian household and took away the life of every firstborn, yet He touched not a soul in the houses of the children of Israel? Do you not know what He did with the Red Sea and Pharaoh's army? Do you not know what He did at the River Jordan and in Jericho? Do you not know what God did to Moses, a man with whom God spoke face-to-face, when he disobeyed Him? Do you not know what He did to Ananias and Sapphira his wife when they lied to the Holy Spirit? Do you not know what He did to Achan and his entire household when he took of the accursed things? Do you not know what He did to His own Son when He (Jesus) became sin for us?

God is trying to tell us something. Are we listening? Do we hear Him speaking? Those who have the Spirit of God hear the Word of God. Turn today from sinful and evil ways and ask God's forgiveness so that you might live as Christ; then God will use you to be the light so that those living in darkness might see, and as salt so that the truth of His Word may cause many to run, saying, "What must I do to be saved?"

The flesh fights against the Spirit of God and the Spirit against the flesh. Each day Christians must choose which one they will follow. To which one will they surrender and allow control of their lives? If we keep ourselves pure, we will be utensils that God can use for His purpose. Our lives will be clean, and we will be ready for the Master to use us for every good work (2 Timothy 2:21 NLT). How we live our lives as Christians before other Christians and the world is important, because how we live testifies to the power of Christ, the reality of His power at work in our lives. The more we live a life that is godly, holy, and pure in Christ, the greater the evidence will be of His power in us, which then manifests itself outside of us for others to see.

If the power of Christ is not able to transform the lives of those who believe (put their trust in Him) to keep them from sinning against God, then it is no power at all. If Christ is powerless to transform our lives now, He is also powerless to raise us from the dead later. Though God knows every man's heart, for a professing Christian who continues living a sinful lifestyle, one contrary to the written word of God, it is questionable whether he ever really came to faith in Jesus Christ. Jesus has the power both to transform (make a sinner a saint-change his heart) and to raise the dead to life. The proof of a Christian's message that Jesus is Lord of his life and that he has been delivered from the power of sin will be manifested by the godly and obedient lifestyle he lives in Christ.

People are looking for miracles today. Let them see one in you. Let them see how God has changed your life and turned it around.

May the Lord help us in this war between our two opposing natures. As the flesh and the Spirit do battle, may He give us the strength to live in the world as one who has been crucified to the flesh, no longer living for self but for Christ. May the Lord's grace abound in our lives so that we may live an abundant life in Christ *For God's Glory.*

CHAPTER 2

GET OUT OF THE ENEMY'S CAMP

For the love of Christ compels us, because
we judge thus: that if One died for all, then
all died; and He died for all, that those who
live should live no longer for themselves, but
for Him who died for them and rose again.
**Therefore, from now on, we regard no one
according to the flesh** (2 Corinthians 5:14-
17, author's emphasis)

What do the words in bold mean to you? Have you ever
read, heard, or considered them, giving them any
thought during your walk with God? A Christian who regards
a brother or sister in Christ in terms of the flesh, in terms of
gender, race, color of skin, or ethnic origin, lacks the evidence
of being a new creation in that area of his life. A gender- and
racially-biased Christian is an oxymoron. Those old things
passed away when he became a new creature in Christ.

The love of God sees beyond all of that; the love of God
gets to the heart of the matter. The love of God that is in

the believer—the love of His Son, His beloved—ought to compel the believer to turn from this evil and do what is right and pleasing in the sight of God. We are to love one another, for love is of God, and all who love are born of God and know God. If we do not love it is because we do not know God, for God is love. "In this the love of God was manifested toward us, that God has sent His only begotten Son into the world, that we might live through Him. In this is love, not that we loved God, but that He loved us and sent His Son to be the propitiation for our sins. Beloved, if God so loved us, we also ought to love one another. No one has seen God at any time. If we love one another, God abides in us, and His love has been perfected in us" (1 John 4:9-12).

Jesus said in Matthew 22:37-38 that this is the first and great commandment, "You shall love the LORD your God with all your heart, with all your soul, and with all your mind." To love the creature whom God has created is to love the Creator. "If we say we love God and hate our brother, we are liars. For if we do not love our brother whom we have seen, how can we love God whom we have not seen? The commandment from Christ is that he who loves God must love his brother also" (1 John 4:20-21). To love our brothers and sisters in Christ is not an option for the children of God. The love of God sees no one's gender or skin color or ethnic heritage as a way to divide and separate but as a means to draw near to God, embracing all whom God has created.

Can we not look at the color of people's skin, the gender that God made them (male and female), hear the language they speak, take no thought of where and how they worship as long as they worship the same Lord God in spirit and in truth, and any other visible attributes, and see the God who created them? Can we not look beyond the person and see the Christ who lives inside the heart? If we cannot, it is because we will not. Therein lies the problem. We have not surrendered our hearts to the will of God in the matter so that

He can fill us with that which is lacking and missing inside. And because we have not surrendered, we do not obey the command to love God with all our heart, soul, and mind. To love God is to obey Him; there is no way around it (see 2 John 5-6).

If we will not love the children of God down here on earth, we will not love them in heaven. If we will not embrace all the children of God now, we will not embrace them in the coming kingdom. If we will not let go of the traditions of our fathers and our worldly ways, it is because of an unrepentant heart. We have not turned from sin (changed our mind about this sin in our lives). Earth is the proving ground. Either we will prove ourselves faithful and obedient now or stand before the Lord later and hear Him say, "Depart from Me, you doer of iniquity." The Christian's life is a test of the will...a test of the heart...a test of obedience.

The one who does the will of God abides forever (1 John 2:17). "Whoever abides in Him does not sin. Whoever sins has neither seen Him nor known Him. Whoever has been born of God does not sin, for His seed remains in him, and he cannot sin, because he has been born of God" (1 John 3:6,9). Be absolutely certain that you have been born again, born of the Spirit of God. Just because someone says "I'm a Christian" does not make it so. Sin for a born-again believer—a child of God—is an exception and not the rule.

The LORD told Moses in Exodus 32:33, "Whoever has sinned against Me, I will blot him out of My book." To which book is God referring? He's referring to the Book of Life, is He not? What God spoke unto Moses was true then and it is just as true today. The truth never changes.

The Lord told Cain in Genesis 4:7, "And if you do not do well, sin lies at the door. And its desire is for you, but you should rule over it." If this sin of racial prejudice and gender bias rules within your heart, if you are a slave to it, confess it and ask God to forgive you; ask God to remove it. If we confess our sins, God is faithful and just to forgive our sins and to cleanse us from all unrighteousness. When true confession is made (telling God the whole truth) and the heart has truly repented of this sin, then God will remove it and cleanse the Christian's heart of unrighteousness.

The children of God are not separated spiritually by the color of their skin or their gender; their lives are hidden in Christ. In Christ they are one body. God is Spirit. The things of God are spiritual. Why are some Christians still living and acting like those without the Spirit of God? Our family business is out in the street. The unbelievers see what we are doing and how we are treating each other, and it gives them cause to blaspheme against our heavenly Father. Jesus said that the world would know that we are His disciples by the love we have for one another. True disciples of Christ no longer live for themselves but for Christ who died for them. The cost to live for and follow Jesus is great. Ninety-nine and a half will not do; we must give up all rights to self. We must give our lives to Him, totally and completely. Anything less is unacceptable.

I recall a conversation I once had with some classmates in junior high school. We talked about several things that day, one of which was religion. I commented to one student that I was going to stop by his church one Sunday and visit. After all, we were friends. This was his response to me: "You can't come to my church." I asked, "Why not?" though I already knew the answer. He told me it was because I was black. He was white.

I could learn with him in the classroom and play together with him on the school grounds, but I could not cross the boundary that man had set by stopping by "his church" to worship with him. Sadly, that is still the way it is in many churches today. God has set no such boundaries. As Jesus told the Samaritan woman at the well, "Woman, believe Me, the hour is coming when you will neither on this mountain nor in Jerusalem, worship the Father. God is Spirit, and those who worship Him must worship in spirit and in truth" (John 4:21, 24). *You stay with your people and I will stay with my people* is, in essence, the message that segregated congregations are sending. Who are your people? Are they not all the children of God, children from all walks of life, all races, creeds, and colors who believe in the Lord Jesus Christ? This church has their God and that church has their God. Is Christ divided? There is only one God, who is the Father of all who believe in Jesus Christ. We find written in Ephesians 4:6 that there is one God and Father of all, who is above all and through all and in all. There is no black church, white church, African church, Hispanic church, or Asian church, etc. In identifying the church in this manner, the focus is on man and not on Christ. We have the church of God spread out over the seven continents. There are Christians in North America and South America, Christians in Africa, Christians in Europe, Asia, etc. The common denominator that bonds them all together is Christ. Their identity is in Christ and Christ alone.

There is only one church of God—the body of Christ that is comprised of believers from all over the world. Because of where God has placed peoples on this earth, the local body of Christ may be of one race or ethnicity or tongue. Although these individuals come together at a manmade structure to worship and serve the Lord, we must remember that God does not dwell in a temple made with hands. And if God desires to send other members into that body, who are they to say, "Not here in this place"? We too often try to fit God into our image, our likeness of what He should be, instead of looking into the perfect law of liberty and being transformed into the likeness and image of His Son.

Of the ten commandments God gave to Moses, the first was this: "You shall have no other gods before Me" (Exodus 20:3). That which we love more than God is an idol in our lives. Idolatry is sin. Racial prejudice and gender bias is sin. It is how those who don't know God through a personal relationship with Christ treat others. We cannot continue treating our brothers and sisters in Christ in this manner and think that God is ignoring our actions. If God judges those outside the family for mistreating His children, will He not also judge those in the family when they mistreat their own? God is a just God and He will judge sin—no matter who sins. How and when God judges sin is entirely up to Him.

Do you love God? Then keep His commandments and obey His Word. Get rid of this sin. We keep looking at Christians through the lens of the world instead of through the eyes of Christ whom we claim to know, follow, and serve. Satan has one mission: to steal, kill, and destroy. Satan knows his end and he wants to take as many folks to hell with him as he can. This sin gives a foothold to Satan in our lives. Satan wants to devour, and he will take every opportunity we give him to destroy us.

Can we not see how Satan, that serpent of old, is using the creature against the Creator? He did it with Adam and Eve in the Garden with a piece of fruit, and he is using racial prejudice and gender bias to break our fellowship with each other and with God today. How long will we continue allowing the devil to use us? Nothing can separate us from the love of God, but sin separates us from God by breaking our communion and fellowship with God. "This is the message which we have heard from Him and declare to you, that God is light and in Him is no darkness at all. If we say that we have fellowship with Him and walk in darkness, we lie and do not practice the truth. But if we walk in the light as He is in the light, we have fellowship with one another, and the blood of Jesus Christ His Son cleanses us from all sin" (1 John 1:5-7).

A Christian cannot draw nigh to God when he is still in the enemy's camp. He cannot fully enjoy fellowship with the Father and the Son as long as he holds onto this sin. As often as we do not welcome all members of God's family into our assembly, we do not welcome Christ. As often as we do it unto the least of these our brethren, we do it unto Christ. We sing these words as we worship God, "Welcome into this place," yet members of His family stand outside our door. The world cannot tell that we are disciples of Christ because we do not show love for all of God's children. We have been commanded by God to submit to Him and to resist the devil so that he will flee. This is one of the wiles (tricks) of the devil. It is used by him to bring division in the church, the body of Christ, the family of God. Has he succeeded in doing this through you?

Because we now belong to God, we are no longer authorized to carry the things that belong to Satan—racism, hatred, partiality, etc. These things are excess baggage. Airlines charge an additional fee for having more bags than you are authorized to carry. We will also pay a price with God if we continue to carry our excess worldly baggage inside the body of Christ.

We must remember that we are engaged in spiritual warfare against the enemies of God. We do not wrestle against flesh and blood, but we wrestle against powers that we cannot see. The children of God are not our enemies; they are members of the family of God, our family. We are not to mistreat, despise, neglect, or treat as inferior any member of the family, nor hate members of the family. "He who says he is in the light, and hates his brother, is in darkness until now. He who loves his brother abides in the light, and there is no cause for stumbling in him. But he who hates his brother is in darkness and walks in darkness, and does not know where he is going, because the darkness has blinded his eyes" (1 John 2:9-11). You must renew your mind according to the truth of God's holy Word in order to prove what is that good and acceptable and perfect will of God. Where is the proof that Jesus is alive and lives in and among us? Where is the love of

Christ for those created in God's image? The Thessalonians had a good record of loving one another as told to us by the Apostle Paul. But Paul urged them to increase in that love more and more. (1 Thessalonians 4:9,10) His message rings loud and clear even to this day. Have we not heard the voice of God on family? Or do we hear His voice yet choose to disobey Him anyway? Let the latter not be so for believers reading this message. It is better not to have heard than to hear and disobey. Do you not believe what God says when He tells you that if you are a friend of the world you are His enemy, so therefore you continue in sin? Unbelief is sin. The time to get out of the enemy's camp is now. We are not at liberty to pick and choose those whom we will love. God commands us to love everybody. We are to love our neighbor as ourselves. We cannot keep saying we are Christians—the children of a God who is love, followers of Jesus Christ—and yet do the works of the enemy. Now is the time to surrender this sin of racial prejudice and gender bias against our brothers and sisters in Christ. If we really believed what the Word of God says, would we honestly continue living the way we do, doing this thing which displeases our heavenly Father?

God is calling those who are His children to start honoring His holy name and to live as He commands. Obedience unto God is not an option for a child of God. God dwells inside of us. We have the power of almighty God at our disposal, and yet we will not acknowledge it and ask God to remove this stain—this sin—from our hearts. Why do we not ask? Could it be because we love doing what we are doing and living the way we are living more than we love God? If it is due to ignorance, then God will not blame us for what we do not know. However, when our lack of knowledge of Christ is due to our own neglect of God's Word, we will be held accountable by God.

Do not take this call of God to righteousness (obedience) lightly. Yes, God understands our frame, that we are nothing but creatures of the dust and that we were born in sin and shaped in iniquity. He understands that before we accepted Christ, everything we learned and were taught came from the devil because we were children of the devil. Now we have no excuse for our sin because He (God) that is in us is greater than he (Satan) that is in the world. We have the One who created us dwelling inside of us, the One who possesses all power in heaven and in the earth in His hands. God wants to show Himself strong on our behalf by removing this sin from our hearts. He wants to show us that this is not an impossible task for Him to do. God wants to give blessings to us, but if we will not surrender this sin to Him, how can He give blessings?

God did not ask us to change our own hearts. It is impossible for us to do so, but not for God. With God all things are possible. He alone can do it. He has the power to deliver. Sanctification is an ongoing process in which the power of God through His Spirit removes the filth and stench that came with us when we accepted Christ as our Savior. This process is necessary so that we can begin to look and smell like Jesus. We came to Jesus just as we were. Now He has to clean us up. But because we refuse to obey God in this matter, we forfeit His blessings, both individually and corporately as a body. When we yield (sow) to the world's customs and traditions, we will receive (reap) some serious spiritual consequences for ourselves. The child of God whom we shun or refuse to love because of gender, race, skin color, language, wealth or poverty, Christian denomination, occupation, or any other criterion of the flesh that we use to sin against God, just may be the very one in whom God has reserved a blessing(s), but we will never receive it because we refuse to get out of the enemy's camp. God told Abram that He would bless those who bless him and curse him who curses him. Are we blessing or cursing the children of Abraham, the family members of God?

Among the children of God who are guilty of this sin, some will come to repentance, confess their sins unto God, and receive His forgiveness. Their works of repentance will evidence it. Others will remain stubborn, stiff-necked, and rebellious and as a result leave God no other choice but to bring the rod of correction against them. God will have to discipline them in love to get them to see the error of their ways. Why? Because when He called, they did not answer. When He spoke, they did not hear but continued to do evil before His eyes and choose that in which He does not delight. There is always a calm before the storm. God is a merciful God, and He gives us a warning to repent and change our sinful ways (change course, change direction) before He brings judgment for our sins.

Narrow is the gate and difficult is the way that leads to eternal life and few find it (Matthew 7:13-14). Are you numbered among the few? To follow Jesus is to abandon the world's ways and the things of the world. Jesus said, "Whoever loses his life for My sake will find it" (Matthew 16:25). Do you see what I see? Do you hear what I hear from the Word of God as to His expectation of those who follow His Son, those who are members of His family?

The earthly family with all of its various relationships began on earth, and it will come to an end on earth. Nothing earthly will enter heaven. (See 1 Corinthians 15:50.) Those born of the flesh are flesh, and those born of the Spirit are spirit. The heavenly family (the spiritual family of God) is called out from among the earthly family. "Therefore come out from among them and be separate, says the Lord" (2 Corinthians 6:17). Those who hear the voice of the Shepherd, Jesus Christ, and respond through faith in Him become members of God's family. This relationship between a people and their God begins on earth but endures throughout eternity. "I will dwell in them and walk among them. I will be their God, and they shall be My people" (2 Corinthians 6:16). Jesus made it quite clear in Mark 3:31-33 who His true family is—His brothers, His sisters, and His mother. They are the ones who do the will of God.

I believe we have too many earthly-minded Christians in the body of Christ. Family relationships on earth are very important. Jesus too had an earthly family. Yet at the age of twelve Jesus was about His Father's business. Jesus understood what we must come to understand. All that we have received from God is a gift. We should not place the gift above the One who gave it. Our families are a gift from God. The gift is to be enjoyed in a manner pleasing to God. However, Christians must not lose sight of the bigger picture: Only those who put their faith in Christ will live with Him in heaven.

"Therefore, my brethren, you also have become dead to the law through the body of Christ, that you may be married to another—to Him who was raised from the dead, that we should bear fruit to God" (Romans 7:4). Jesus Christ was the first fruit among many. Christ is married to the church. The church is His bride. In terms of the spiritual relationship between Christ and His bride, the church is the mother of all who believe in Christ. Jesus told Peter, "Upon this rock I will build my church and the gates of hell shall not prevail against it." God seeks godly offspring. The seed of Christ, which is the Word of God, fathers the children of God by the power of the Holy Spirit. Jesus said that no one can come to Him unless the Father draws him. The Father by His Spirit brings lost souls to Jesus His Son through His Word. The Word of God goes out into the world, and the Spirit of life convicts men's hearts of sin by the Word they hear. Once convicted, the one who hears will either believe and repent or not believe and continue in sin.

31

Believers are to abide in Christ so that they may bear fruit and multiply. One believer plants the seed and another waters the seed, but God gives the increase. Without Jesus Christ we can do nothing, for He speaks the words of God. Jesus alone has the words that give eternal life (John 6:68-69). "For I am not ashamed of the gospel of Christ, for it is the power of God to salvation for everyone who believes, for the Jew first and also for the Greek. For in it the righteousness of God is revealed from faith to faith; as it is written, 'The just shall live by faith'" (Romans 1:16-17). Faith comes by hearing and hearing by the Word of God. Heaven and earth will pass away, but God's Word will last forever. Those born of that Word, that seed of Christ, will not perish but live forever. The Word will remain, and those born of the Word will also remain.

The children of God are children through faith.

> For you are all sons of God through faith in Christ Jesus. For as many of you as were baptized into Christ have put on Christ. There is neither Jew nor Greek, there is neither slave nor free, there is neither male nor female; for you are all one in Christ Jesus. And if you are Christ's, then you are Abraham's seed, and heirs according to the promise.
>
> Galatians 3:26-29

If we abide in Christ and Christ in us, we will bear much fruit. A man is joined to his wife and the two become one. Their fruit is the offspring between them. There will be no need for marriages in heaven outside of the one between Christ and His bride, because all of the godly offspring will have been produced on earth (see Matthew 22:29-30). What Adam and Eve failed in doing (to produce godly offspring in their union), Christ and the church will succeed in doing *For God's Glory*.

Adam's seed is the seed of death. For by one man's disobedience, all have sinned. The wages of sin is death. Christ's seed is the seed of life. For by one Man's obedience, many will be made righteous (placed in right standing with God, declared not guilty of sin). **Notice I did not say that all will be made righteous by Christ's obedience as in Adam all have sinned because of his disobedience. We had no choice in being born in sin. We have a choice in being born again. We have a choice to either repent (stop sinning) and believe or not repent and keep on sinning. Those who choose not to repent but to continue in sin are those who will not be made righteous by Christ's obedience.**

The Apostle Paul writes of walking properly toward those who are outside. (1 Thessalonians 4:12) We must be careful how we live before the unsaved members of our earthly family and the rest of the world. They need to see Jesus and hear Jesus and witness His power in our lives if we are to have any hope of them coming to Him for their salvation. Why did Jesus die? To take away the sin of the world, yes, but ultimately for the glory of God. Why must Christians die? For this same reason, for the glory of God. As Jesus died to save the world, Christians must die to self in order for Christ to live through them so that the Father may draw those who are dead in trespasses and sins to Himself. If Jesus is lifted up, He will draw all peoples to Himself. The believer's body is the temple of the Spirit of God. It is through this temple that God has chosen to work in order to save the lost in this world.

We must die to this world's ways in order to live for Christ. The more attached we become to Christ, the less attached we become to the world. Cling to Jesus and never let Him go. Who would forfeit eternal life for the temporary pleasures of sin? For the sake of Christ and in honor of His holy name, let us stop allowing the enemy to use us. Let us get out of his camp. We must let go of tradition and old habits and let go of sin in order for others to see the new life bought with the blood of Christ that we have received.

Lord, make us, Your children, increase and abound in love to one another and to all, so that You may establish our hearts blameless in holiness before our God and Father at the coming of our Lord Jesus Christ with all His saints.

CHAPTER 3

PRETENDING SUBMISSION
TO GOD

Follow me to a place that is a grand banquet hall, unlike any place you have seen or could ever imagine here on earth. I have no words to describe it other than it is absolutely breathtaking. Gathered together inside are people from every tongue and every nation, every race/creed/color. They have come from every part of the world to take their places in the kingdom of God. They are there by invitation only. Some were young, some were old, and some were in between when they accepted the invitation. Some held on to that invitation for a few years and others for many, many years…some perhaps only for a few days or weeks. They held that invitation through faith.

They have all come together now to receive the promise. It is a wedding celebration. The host is none other than the Bridegroom, the Lord Jesus Christ. The guests are all dressed in white. There isn't one spot or wrinkle present. They are His bride. Those deemed worthy are now walking with Him in white, those whose names were never erased from the Book of Life. Those who held fast to their belief in Christ,

35

those who kept the faith, those who endured the race until the end, those who loved God and obeyed His command-ments (kept His Word), those who believed and lived by the Word of God and not the words of man—they are the ones who now celebrate. This is the reward for their faith: to be with Christ, to be joined to Him as one forever.

As you look out among the people who are there with the Lord, do you see your face? Did you make it in? Through faith in Christ, do you see yourself there, present and accounted for? No man knows, but God knows for certain, if the man or woman who professes to be a Christian will make it in. We can fool others and ourselves with pious acts and good works, but not God. We appear godly to man, but our hearts may be far from God. We ought to know, however, as professing Christians whether or not we have truly repented and asked Christ into our hearts, whether or not we have the Spirit of God dwelling inside us, whether or not we truly believe in Jesus Christ. God gives His Spirit to all believers as a guarantee of eternal life. If you know that you have God's Spirit, then you know that you are His and He will keep all who belong to Him until the end.

Sadly, all who say they are Christians will not be there to celebrate the wedding of the Lamb of God and His bride. We have some double agent Christians among us—those pretending submission. They are professors, yet they do not possess Christ. The evidence is in the life they live. They profess to believe, but they do not live their lives according to the Word of God. They do not trust that God's Word is absolute truth so they have added to or taken away from the Word of God.

They profess Christ yet do the works of the devil. Their fruit is not good fruit. They go through the motions of being saved, acting as though they have received Christ for salva-tion, but in due time, when the time is fulfilled, God will reveal the true sheep of His pasture, for God alone knows a man's heart. "I'm not so bad" some say when they compare themselves to others. How quickly they forget that God is not comparing the life they live against others. God is measuring their lives against His holy Word. (Hebrews 4:12) This is why it is important to understand that the only One after whom Christians should pattern their lives is Christ.

A false Christian is likened to a pig that returns to the mud after it is clean or a dog that returns to its vomit. He eventually shows his true nature. A false Christian is one who has no fear of God. He uses God's name in vain and shakes his fist in the face of God as he defies God's Word and His will by playing the harlot with the enemies of God. A false Christian is an adulterer/adulteress. A false Christian worships man as God. Those pretending submission have not completely returned to God.

A true Christian, on the other hand, reveres God and stands in awe of His name and is one who does not sin (willfully or continually) against God. A true Christian sees God's Word as the highest authority and it is His Word and His Word alone to which he clings. A true Christian is one who looks into the face of Christ and sees the light and he welcomes the light so that the darkness in his own life has to flee. He cannot look into the light and practice evil (practice sinning against God) at the same time.

We must be absolutely certain today that we have received life by the Spirit of God. The Word of God is the key to life. It's elementary: If we repent, ask Jesus to forgive our sins and to come into our hearts, and believe that He is there (faith) , we will receive life. The evidence of our belief is in our obedience. Our obedience leads to spiritual growth/ maturity, which in turn leads to good works/producing fruit for God. All of this is done by the grace of God. If we obey, then we are blessed.

Let us live our life down here as though we are the bride dressed in white. Let nothing—absolutely nothing—stain, spoil, or ruin the spotless garment of righteousness that we have received from Christ. Let us keep ourselves unspotted from the world.

At no time has God commanded us to be sinless (without sin), for our natural birth ruled that out. Only one Man met that perfect standard—Jesus. God does, however, command us to obey His Word and live in submission to His Son's authority. The more we put on the righteousness of Christ (moral and ethical correct actions/behavior), the less we will sin. God promises that the one who hungers and thirsts for righteousness shall be filled. (Matthew 5:6) The closer we get to God, the farther away we get from sin. **A Christian puts distance between himself and sin in order to have no distance (no break in fellowship) between himself and God.**

"Blessed are all who hear the word of God and put it into practice" (Luke 11:28 NLT). Do not take offense to what is written, but rather try to understand what the Word of God is saying. If we take offense to God's Word down here, God knows we will be offended in heaven. God's Word will last forever. If we will not receive and obey the truth down here, we will not receive and obey it in heaven. Either we have faith in Christ (total belief in God's Word) or we do not. To believe in Christ is to turn away from sin—to stop doing that which displeases God. Partial belief is really unbelief. Partial compliance is really noncompliance. Do not misunderstand the righteousness of God. God is holy, and nothing unclean, vile, wicked, or evil—no sin—will dwell in His holy presence. Holiness adorns God's house forever. If God forsook (turned away from) His own Son, the One whom He loved and who pleased Him when Jesus carried upon His body all the world's sin, do you honestly think that God is going to let a man or woman waltz into heaven, eat of the wedding feast, and sit among the saints when he or she has not met God's righteous requirement (that which we must do to be in right standing with Him)...to repent and believe in His Son?

Do not be deceived for God is not mocked; whatever we sow, that we shall also reap (Galatians 6:7). God cannot look upon us either if we are not wearing the righteousness of God in Christ. Those without the wedding garment will be cast into outer darkness (Matthew 22:11-14).

Lay down your sins. Do whatever you must to keep your entire body from hell. Pluck out your right eye or cut off your right hand if they cause you to sin against God. Let go of any practice or activity that is sin (Matthew 5:29-30). Each time you sin and you know you have sinned yet you continue doing the thing habitually, then it is disobedience and rebellion against God, and these are signs of an unbelieving heart. You do not really believe that Jesus is coming back unexpectedly. You do not believe that you dishonor God's holy name before His enemies when you sin. You do not believe that Jesus is who He says He is. You do not believe that God has determined the number of your days and your soul could be required of you this very moment. You play Russian roulette with sin.

We all start out the same in this life—born in sin. But we will not all finish this life the same—saved by the blood of Christ from the wrath of God—because all will not believe in Jesus' name; all will not submit to His authority. All authority in heaven and on earth has been given to Jesus (Matthew 28:18). Do you know what that means? It means that Jesus has the authority to allow a man in the kingdom of God or to keep him out. It is that simple. Be very careful how you treat Jesus. Be very careful of what you say, where you go, and what you do while using His holy name. Be very certain that you are a child of God, a true Christian and not a pretender..

Try to imagine being in a place that you can never leave (hell). Now try to imagine being in a place that you would never want to leave (heaven). At the end of this life one of those two places will be your eternal dwelling place. Once you check in, you can never check out (see Luke 16:26). We cannot see heaven nor can we see hell with our natural eyes. By faith one believes in the reality of both places according to what the Word of God says concerning them. They are real; they both exist. And if one truly believes, he lives his life accordingly. He will live a life of faith in Christ that pleases God in order to go to heaven. Or he will refuse to believe and destroy himself by continuing a life of sin (rebellion) against a holy and just God and go to hell. Man chooses the lifestyle—one of rebellion or repentance unto God. God chooses the final destination. Those who hear the gospel of Christ make the choice now as to which place God will send them by the kind of life they live before God—either in Christ or outside of Christ.

Jesus Himself was under the covenant. He chose life by keeping God's commands, laws, and regulations, by walking in God's ways. Jesus pleased God because He knew what was right and He chose to do it, and He knew what was wrong and He rejected it. Because Jesus did that, He received life. His sacrifice for you and for me was acceptable unto God because He lived a life without spot or blemish—the perfect Lamb. Jesus lived a life of perfect obedience. And God gave Jesus the power and authority to give life to all who follow Him. You must submit to God if you want to see God. If you are not committed and devoted to God (the ways of God, the things of God, the Word of God), then you have not submitted to God. You and God alone know if you are pretending submission to Him.

"I have stretched out My hands all day long to a rebellious people, who walk in a way that is not good, according to their own thoughts" (Isaiah 65:2). God did all He could to bring the children of Israel back to Him. He kept sending the prophets with a word from Him, pleading with them. He poured out His love toward them, but they thought it a small thing to hear and to obey. They refused to listen and turn from their wicked ways. The underlying cause behind all of their wickedness, unfaithfulness, and their adulterous relationships with false gods was their unbelief. They had not been humbled (broken in heart) nor had they feared God. The children of Israel told Jeremiah, "As for the word that you have spoken to us in the name of the Lord, we will not listen to you! But we will certainly do whatever has gone out of our own mouth" (Jeremiah 44:16-17).

This is the same attitude some Christians have today. There is nothing new under the sun. This is in essence what they also say to God when they hear the Word and turn deaf ears, or when they hear the Word and refuse to obey (refuse to repent). The preacher stands before them Sunday after Sunday, and Wednesday after Wednesday, preaching the truth and teaching them "thus says the Lord," straight from the Word of God. And they keep coming Sunday after Sunday and Wednesday after Wednesday, but there is no change in how they live. Some remain that same old ornery person; that same old mean-spirited Christian; that same old gossiper; that same old liar; that same old fornicator/adulterer; that same old slacker who sits down on God and will not do things in the church to serve God through His people; that same old non-tithes-paying Christian; that same old Christian who complains about every little thing; that same old grudge carrier, refusing to let go of the past and forgive others who have wronged him; that same old man trying to defend his manhood—not going to let anybody punk him out or get the best of him or think that he is weak—so he avenges himself of the wrong that was done...he will not wait on God to do it. He will not let go of the old things, the old ways, and the old habits...the old man. He clings to these old things as if they contain life. They do not; they contain only death. He will not allow the Word to change his heart, "for with the heart one believes unto righteousness" (Romans 10:10). Our heart is the source of our motivations. Therefore, we are motivated to righteousness or unrighteousness. A good man out of the good treasure of his heart brings forth good; and an evil man out of the evil treasure of his heart brings forth evil. (Luke 6:45)

We enter the covenant by God's grace (kindness) through faith—by believing the Word of God—and we remain in the covenant by faith until the end. Abraham believed (faith) the Lord and He accounted it to him for righteousness (Genesis 15:6). By entering into the covenant, God confirms that you are His child and He is your God. When you entered into the covenant with God, you also agreed to accept His judgment if you broke the covenant whether you realized or knew this truth or not. You willingly gave God your word, your solemn promise to keep the covenant... that is, to turn from sin (to repent). God wants you to come clean—uphold your obligations—and do what you said you would do before it is too late. Let your yes be yes and your no be no...no middle ground. **Let no one who reads this message consider himself/herself immune, thinking, "I am safe, even though I am walking in my own stubborn way" (Deuteronomy 29:19).** Let none consider themselves safe because they go into the chapel, the church, or the sanctuary on Sundays. Do not fool yourselves by thinking that you can continue living in sin and then come to church, singing worship and praise songs, putting your money in the offering plate, serving on this board and that board, this committee and that committee, and then leave and return to your sinful lifestyle and God is pleased.

Why will you not submit to God? Why will you not resist the devil? Are you spending time with the enemy in order to witness to him...to try to convert him? If it is not that, then what is the reason? What other possible reason could you have for hanging out with Satan, the enemy of God? He is also your enemy. He is your accuser. He does not love or care about you. Satan wants to destroy you.

The covenant obligations are not too difficult to understand and perform. The only obstacle that is preventing us from living as God requires is ourselves. Self is in the way. We cannot keep using the sinful nature excuse. Believers are born again. They have a new way of life because of the life of Christ that has been given to them. Think about it. We have direct access to God in Christ and Christ alone. No man (no human being) can give us direct access to God. We have the power of God in us through the Holy Spirit. We have the words of life. We have available to us all that belongs to Christ as a joint heir. We have power over sin. God offers us every resource necessary to live a godly, obedient, holy, and honorable life before Him. We simply choose not to use what God has supplied. That choice will cost us dearly in the end if we do not hear now and obey.

We have no valid reason or excuse from God's perspective to continue living contrary to His Word. God said that greater is He (Jesus) that is in us than he (Satan) that is in the world. God said that we can do all things through Christ who strengthens us. The Lord told Jeremiah, "Behold, I am the Lord, the God of all flesh. Is there anything too hard for Me?" (Jeremiah 32:26). If these words are not the truth, then they are a lie. **We know that God speaks only the truth from Numbers 23:19, "God is not a man, that He should lie, nor a son of man, that He should repent. Has He said, and will He not do? Or has He spoken, and will He not make it good?"** Our attitude must be a "Christ can do" attitude. It is all about appropriating the power of Christ that we have in us over the sin nature. Christ is able to do exceedingly abundantly above all that we can ask or imagine according to the power that works in us. Christ wants to show Himself strong on behalf of those whose hearts are loyal to Him. **Christians must seek understanding and wisdom from God on how to exercise the power of God within them in order to defeat sin.** Wisdom is the principal thing, therefore get wisdom. But in all our getting, we must get understanding. "The Lord looks down from heaven upon the children of men, to see if there are any who understand, who seek God" (Psalm 14:2). Keep asking, seeking, and knocking. How much more will our heavenly Father give the Holy Spirit to those who ask Him?

O child of God, wake up and start believing by living out the Word of God in your life, and when you do you will begin to experience the power of God in your life. Think about the greater works of harvesting souls for God's kingdom that Jesus talked about. Jesus raised dead physical bodies back to life in order to show that the Father had given Him this power and authority. They eventually died again. We, those who believe, with Christ's power working in us and through us today can help bring dead spirits (the spirits in unbelievers) all over the world to life eternal by the Word and the Spirit of God because God is in the believer wherever he may be in the world. The man or woman whose spirit is born again will never perish. We must realize that this is not about us. It is all about God...it is all for God...it is all *For God's Glory*. We are the vessels through which God wants to work to tell others the good news of salvation. Give God a chance to show Himself faithful on this pilgrim's journey.

The day is coming when all the earth will know that the Lord has done what He purposed: He has fulfilled His Word which He commanded in days of old (Lamentations 2:17). For all creation is waiting eagerly for the future day when God will reveal who His children really are (Romans 8:19 NLT). "On the day when I act, they will be my own special treasure. I will spare them as a father spares an obedient and dutiful child. **Then you will again see the difference between the righteous and the wicked, between those who serve God and those who do not**" (Malachi 3:18-19 NLT).

In Noah's day the rain came and the earth was flooded. The rain destroyed all living things on the earth except Noah, his family of seven, and the animals taken aboard the ark. It happened just as God said it would (Genesis 7:21-23). Do you believe this? In Moses' day, none of the Israelites who rebelled against God when He commanded them to go in and possess the land flowing with milk and honey lived to see the good land God had promised. They all died in the wilderness. It happened just as God said it would. Do you believe this? Now consider this: In each instance of judgment, God spared only a few souls. The gate to eternal life is narrow and there are few who will find it. God truly means what He says and God truly says what He means. God is pleading with you today to turn away from evil—to turn away from ungodliness and uncleanness, to turn away from sin and rebellion (no matter how small or trivial you think it is)—and come to Him and love Him as He has loved you. God spared not the unbelievers (sinners) before Christ, and God will not spare the unbelievers in the coming Day of Judgment—those who "trampled the Son of God underfoot, counted the blood of the covenant by which he was sanctified a common thing, and insulted the Spirit of grace" (Hebrews 10:29). God loves everyone but only the righteous (those who believe in Jesus Christ) shall see Him. Only the righteous shall be saved and dine with Christ in heaven.

In Mary's day a Child was born unto her while she was still a virgin. The Child was conceived by the Spirit of God. The Child was named Jesus, the One who saves. Jesus lived in total submission and obedience to God. He died a horrible death for your sins and mine on the cross at Cavalry. On the third day God raised Jesus to life. After forty days Jesus ascended to heaven where He is now seated at the right hand of the Father, just as God said. Do you believe this? One day Jesus is going to return. "For the Lord Himself will descend from heaven with a shout, with the voice of an archangel, and with the trumpet of God" (1 Thessalonians 4:16). He will come at an unexpected hour…like a thief in the night

(Luke 12:40; 2 Peter 3:10). Christ will take with Him those and only those who belong to Him. Do you believe this? If the answer is yes, then why do you not live as though you believe? If you make it in and you stand before Christ in judgment, will you reap a great reward when He evaluates your works (not works for salvation but works as a result of salvation) because you were faithful and obedient and sowed much that pleased God...because you did the works God prepared for you before the world was created? Or will you be ashamed because many of your works will be burned in the fire because they were done while pretending submission to God?

If you are pretending submission to God, you are headed for ruin and destruction. If you have not figured out by now that this covenant is serious business and that it means a lot to God, then God have mercy on your soul. God's judgment of sin does not always come swiftly, because He is longsuffering and full of mercy, but it always comes. Those pretending submission will reap the spiritual consequences of their sin when they stand before Christ.

Let us not end up like the multitude that wandered for forty years in the wilderness and in the end received their just reward. When God got sick and tired of being sick and tired of His rebellious people, He did what He said He would do. **Though God fed them each day, provided for their every need, took care of them (for forty years their clothes and sandals did not wear out, neither did their feet swell), protected them, and loved them, yet God judged them for their sins. They did not enter the Promised Land (see 1 Corinthians 10:1-11).**They enjoyed God's unmerited favor and gave Him nothing in return. God was faithful to Israel, yet Israel was not faithful to God. After all God did for them, they refused to trust Him...they refused to believe. **God's mercy and His love will not negate/cancel His righteous judgment of sin against Him.**

Are you receiving from God yet not bearing any fruit for Him? Do you continue in sin in spite of all that God has done for you and in spite of His warning to repent, believe, and receive? Has God been faithful to you yet you are not being faithful to Him? Though we are faithless, God remains faithful. He cannot deny Himself (2 Timothy 2:13). What more must God do to get you to submit—to commit, to surrender to Him, to devote yourself to obeying His Word, to stop pretending submission to Him?

CHAPTER 4

THE ROAD TO SALVATION

D o you have a passion for something that you do for the Lord? Mine is writing. I love to write about God, the Word of God, and the things of God. It is a God-given passion because all good and perfect gifts come from God. I must confess that I never really enjoyed reading books until I began reading the sixty-six books of the Bible, the inspired Word of God. The Bible has become my greatest treasure on earth. It contains the wisdom and knowledge of God. In it lies insight into the mind of God. In it lies the secret things of God that are hidden from the wise and the prudent. In it lie the words of life.

Oftentimes God's Word takes hold of me and I do not want to pull away. Have you ever had that happen? Ever find yourself in that state—consumed—just taken over by the Word of God? It is constantly on your mind—morning, noon, and night. For those of you who have, I hope you would agree that it is indeed a wonderful experience that leads to a wonderful life in the Lord. The joy and peace that it gives the believer is beyond explanation. For those who have not and desire it, be patient through obedience, and ask, seek, and knock. God will hear, and He will do what you ask.

The Word of God assures us that if we draw near to God, He will draw near to us.

I began this writing as a very simple explanation of repentance leading to salvation. I wrote it to bring understanding of the truth that without repentance—true repentance—there can be no salvation. However, the simple explanation grew into a work of multiple pages that briefly highlighted such areas as redemption, grace, faith, regeneration, etc. Therefore on the advice and recommendation of Chaplain (MAJ) Connors, the U.S. Army chaplain under whom I served while stationed in Camp Casey, South Korea, I decided to change direction. His comment was, "You are not doing them justice." If it is the Lord's will, future works will address in greater depth separation from God, repentance to life, faith, regeneration (new birth), baptism, grace, fruit/works, just to name a few. What you are reading is a condensed version of the original product.

May God's holy Word and the power of the Holy Spirit help us remain steadfast on the road to salvation. May we be ever so mindful that believers have a good thing in Jesus Christ. For there is none good but God. What believers have is so good that the best is yet to come. Jesus is saving the absolute best for those who keep the faith, those who endure until the end. Let us now walk this road to salvation together.

In the Beginning Sin Separated God and Man

"Then God looked over all he had made, and he saw that it was excellent in every way" (Genesis 1:31 NLT). The 1994 edition of *Webster's II New Riverside University Dictionary* defines excellent as "exceptionally good of its kind; superior."

Everything in the beginning was good (perfect)—God's creation and His relationship with those whom He created. The hearts of Adam and Eve were perfect; their hearts were right in the sight of God. But in one act of rebellion, sin

50

entered the heart of man, and God's perfect creation—all that was exceptionally good—was changed. The serpent deceived Eve, and Adam willfully disobeyed God when they ate of the fruit from the tree of the knowledge of good and evil. God knew Adam would one day disobey Him. In His instructions to Adam God told him, "For in the day that you eat of it you shall surely die" (Genesis 2:17). When we sin (rebel against, disobey God), it is the evidence that we are indeed descendants of Adam. Adam and Eve's sin caused all of mankind to live spiritually separated from God and to die a physical death. The sin of Adam and Eve ushered in death (both spiritual and physical). They were banished from the Garden of Eden, from God's presence (spiritual death). God would no longer walk in the garden in the cool of the day and talk with them, and they eventually died a physical death. Adam lived for 930 years and then he died (Genesis 5:5). Judgment came just as God said it would.

The wages (cost/penalty) of sin is death. Death comes to everyone because of sin. But God, in His eternal love, mercy, and wisdom, had a plan for reconciliation between Himself and mankind. When God created mankind it was personal. God said, "Let Us make man in Our image, according to Our likeness." Then God took in His hands the dust of the earth and created man from it. And with His own mouth He blew into his nostrils the breath of life. And because God loved His handiwork so much—that which He so beautifully and wonderfully made—and desired a relationship that would last forever, He sent His only begotten Son (Jesus Christ) to die for us, to redeem us from the power of sin, which is death. God hates sin. We all have sinned against God and fall short of His glory. We are all deserving of death.

Ugly Is Sin

"God don't like ugly." These are words I would often hear my mother say when referring to the wrong or evil that someone had done. At that time I did not equate "ugly" to sin. I could not until I realized (was made conscious of the fact) later in life that I was a sinner. "And when He *(Holy Spirit)* has come, He will convict the world of sin, and of righteousness, and of judgment: of sin, because they do not believe in Me."

I needed conviction that I was a sinner and that I needed Christ as my Savior. Before conviction, as far as I was concerned, I did something wrong and I knew that the thing was wrong. Not sin—just wrong. So what? If I got away with it, who cared? There were no consequences to worry about, or so I thought. How wrong I was. The One who cared was God. Because of His grace, He cared enough to be patient and show mercy toward me long enough until I repented and changed from my evil ways, until I came to my senses after hearing the gospel, until I believed in Jesus. Before 1997, I was listening to the gospel in church during my sporadic attendance on Sundays but not hearing its message to repent and obey God. What I was hearing was the voice of the evil one (Satan) telling me to come back after church service was over and continue the dance with him—to continue doing that which was ugly. Faith comes by hearing and hearing by the Word of God. When I finally heard the Word of God—when I finally heard His voice—it opened my eyes to the reality of this truth: The wrong (the evil I had been doing) was sin. The One whom I sinned against was God. The life that I lived was a life opposed to God's ways and God's authority. I was a child of the devil, enjoying the sinful pleasures of the flesh, and my sins had me traveling on the broad road of destruction, the wrong road with a one-way ticket to hell. The consequences of my sins, had I not changed direction by the grace of God, would have been eternal damnation if the number of my days ended while I was living a sinful/rebellious lifestyle. How I thank God for His grace and mercy.

God did not like ugly (sin) then, and I believe He hates it even more so now that I profess Christ as Lord and Savior, now that I have entered into the covenant with Him through the blood of His Son. This ought to be every Christian's response to sin: "It is ugly and I cannot bear to look upon sin as my Father in heaven cannot." We are to hate sin as God hates sin.

God Punishes Sin

God makes it clear in His Word for those who will hear that sin will not go unpunished; it comes with a price. "Behold, all souls are Mine; the soul of the father as well as the soul of the son is Mine; the soul who sins shall die" (Ezekiel 18:4). God also makes it clear in His Word that sins forgiven by Him will not be remembered (Isaiah 43:25). Some grab hold of and embrace these truths when they hear them. They believe them, and they sincerely try to live a life in Christ that is pleasing to God. Others are slow in hearing and believing, so they continue in sin. The question the sinning Christian asks, in essence, when he hears a word from the Lord to repent (to stop sinning) yet continues in sin is this, "Who is the Lord that I should obey His voice to let sin go? I do not know the Lord, nor will I let sinful pleasures go!" This same rebellious attitude got Pharaoh in big trouble—he and all of the Egyptians. Sin not only affects the one who sins but others in his life as well. The consequences can be far-reaching. For King David, though he was a man after God's own heart and God forgave him of all the wrong he had done, the sword never left his household.

God has done the same with us as He did with Adam and Eve. God has put us here on this earth and given us instructions on how to live. He never changes. He allows us to exercise our will to live how we choose to live. We can either live in obedience (submission) or disobedience (rebellion). Those are our only two choices. God has established a boundary for us just as He did with Adam and Eve. God loves us, but when we transgress His commandments (cross the line), we leave Him no other choice than to bring discipline/judgment. God does not expect perfection from fallen creatures. We never will or ever can be perfect as long as we possess a sinful nature. We will always be prone to sin as long as we remain in our present bodies. We were conceived in sin and we are by nature sinful people—all people of every nation. Therefore, believers must continually strive to sin less, one day at a time, with the help of God. What God commands is obedience to His Word. His grace abounds toward those who choose to live to please Him. His holy Word is filled with examples (lessons learned for our benefit). A lot of the lessons we learn through personal experience could be avoided if we would take heed to the lessons biblical history has already taught us. Too often we repeat the mistakes of those who have gone on before us because we do not read God's Word (lack of knowledge on our part) and apply it in our lives. We do not heed God's warnings and instructions.

We all must understand that no one can sin with impunity (exemption from punishment). God will punish sin. His holy and just nature will not allow Him to do otherwise. Paul writes in 1 Corinthians 10:12, "Therefore let him who thinks he stands take heed lest he fall." Christians should not be of the mindset that just because they have been justified by God (declared not guilty of sin), nothing will happen to them when they sin against God. Those who do so are playing with fire and they will get burned. If we sow to the flesh, we will reap corruption. We will not escape the judgment that comes to those who practice sin. We must serve God with reverence and godly fear, for He is a consuming fire.

Repent and Live

A man hears the gospel. He hears a voice that says, "This is the way, turn around and walk here." He either responds to the message by coming to Christ or he continues on the path he is traveling, the path of destruction and utter ruin.

God commands all men everywhere to repent, because He has appointed a day on which He will judge the world in righteousness by the Man (Jesus) whom He has ordained. He has given assurance of this to all by raising Him from the dead (Acts 17:30-31). No one can defy God, sin against Him, and get away with it. Repent means repent—not pretend repentance, not quitting for a time and then going back to practicing evil and doing wickedness before the eyes of the Lord. To repent means to have a change of mind about sin. True repentance involves a turning away from sin. A repentant heart stops sinning, stops living a sinful lifestyle. Luke 3:8 (NLT) records John the Baptist telling the people to prove by the way they live that they really had turned from their sins and turned to God.

When a person has a spiritual encounter with Christ, he will know it. It may not be a burning bush experience like Moses had or a Damascus Road experience like Paul had, but it will be one that will change his life. He will confess that he has sinned against God; he will forsake sin (turn away from it and stop living an immoral and ungodly life-style). He will turn to God, and he will begin to walk in the Lord's presence as he lives here on earth, living his life according to the Word of God.

A repentant heart is one that is directed toward God, one that has returned to God, one that serves and follows Christ. A repentant heart is one that is sorrowful for the sins committed against God. A repentant heart honors the name of Christ by doing what is right in the sight of God. A repentant heart gives Christ the best it has to offer for He is a great King. He is the King of kings. A repentant heart is one that loves Christ by doing what He says. A repentant heart is a humble heart, one that is dependent on God. A repentant heart no longer lives to please self but to please Christ who

55

died and was raised for him. A repentant heart is one that fears (reveres, respects) God. A repentant heart is one that loves to think about God and heaven. A repentant heart is one that abides in Christ (habitually obeys Him). A repentant heart no longer participates in the things that immoral, greedy, and impure people do. "For though your hearts were once full of darkness, now you are full of light from the Lord, and your behavior should show it! For this light within you produces only what is good and right and true" (Ephesians 5:8-9 NLT). We should see the evidence (the fruit) on the outside of the work the Holy Spirit is doing on the inside of a repentant heart.

Those who sin against God are guilty. The guilty will not go unpunished. It is a foolish mistake to say that you have repented (turned from evil toward God) and then turn back the other way toward evil (turn your back to God). **The most dangerous position that any man can find himself in is with his back turned to almighty God.** Will a man go back on his word, his oath that he made with God when he entered the blood covenant of Christ? Does he think he can get away with it or escape judgment? Hear the message from the Old Testament that God gave Nahum concerning the Assyrians in Nineveh: "You will have no more children to carry on your name. I will destroy all the idols in the temples of your gods. I am preparing a grave for you because you are despicable and don't deserve to live!" (Nahum 1:14 NLT). "'I am your enemy!' says the Lord Almighty" (Nahum 2:13 NLT). Remember how the people of Nineveh repented when they heard the message from the Lord that Jonah preached? God relented from the disaster that He said He would bring upon them, and He did not do it (Jonah 3:7-10). The Ninevites were saved from God's divine punishment because they believed the Word of God and turned from evil. Sadly, however, the city fell back into wickedness. Its repentance was short-lived; the people returned to their sin. Many years later God sent

Babylon to destroy Nineveh (read Nahum 1-3). It matters not if many sin against God or just one sins against God. He will judge sin. Believe me, it is much better if God uses His power for you than against you.

Can you hear the voice of God, professing Christians? Can you hear God telling you not to take repentance lightly? Can you hear Jesus telling you that if you love Him you will obey His commands? The Lord is trying to tell you something. Do you hear Him? If not, then perhaps you are not His. Jesus said that His sheep hear His voice. If you know you have not truly repented, then do so before it is too late. Consider what you forfeit by sinning against God. When Esau sold his birthright for one morsel of food, he was later rejected when he wanted to inherit the blessing. He found no place for repentance though he sought it diligently with tears.

Do you not see how faith in Jesus through obedience brings eternal life? When you obey Jesus, you remain in His love. Jesus remained in His Father's love because Jesus obeyed Him. Your love for Christ will show itself in obedience to the Word of God. If you love Jesus then obey His Word. If you obey His Word then you will not live in sin. If you do not live in sin, then you will have fellowship with God. If you have fellowship with God, then you are His and He will keep/preserve you until the end. The evidence of your salvation will show itself in the lifestyle you live.

If you say you are a Christian, are you living as though you truly are? Those who live in sin deny Christ. They live as though they don't know Him. How can a Christian living a sinful lifestyle hope to convince an unbeliever that Jesus is real—that his sins have been forgiven? A Christian living a sinful lifestyle is an unbelievable witness for Christ. Jesus Christ enters a man's heart to change it, to give him a new heart. Repentance is an enduring reality that is seen by others who are witness to the kind of life we live. O child of God, the unbelievers will come (be drawn to Christ) when they see that the Lord our God is with us. How will they see? By the Christlike way we live.

Ruth told Naomi that Naomi's people would be her people and Naomi's God her God. There must have been something about Naomi's people and her God that caused Ruth to leave her homeland and her false gods. There also ought to be something that an unbeliever sees in the life of a believer that will cause him to leave his father, the devil, and choose the God of heaven as his Father. There should be something in the life of a believer that will cause the unbeliever to choose the people of God as his people.

Perhaps the underlying issue here is that you have never really died to sin if you are one who continues in sin, doing things that displease God. To willfully sin against God after you have told Him you are His is a violation of trust. He is a jealous God and He will not share your love with His enemy. You sleep with the devil and then offer your defiled body to God. It is an offering that God will certainly refuse. **A Christian living in sin can only present a body that is defiled, unholy, and unacceptable to God.**

He hangs out with the devil during the week and then shows up for church on Sunday morning as if nothing has happened—as if all is well between him and God. He still smells of the devil's cologne. It is not a sweet-smelling aroma unto God. It is a stench in His nostrils. Do you think God forgives only certain sins and ignores others? Consider the foolishness of your actions. Consider the outcome of your conduct. You stand in the gallows with a noose around your neck (that noose being your sins), not knowing when the signal will be given for the hangman to pull the lever. Consider even more so the holiness of God. His holiness will not allow sin in His presence. Holiness signifies separation to God. When a man lives in sin, he lives an unholy and ungodly lifestyle and that man is separated from God. If you say you have fellowship with God but are walking in darkness, then you are a liar. It is a sad commentary for a Christian to have the light in him yet walk in darkness. The light is hidden because he cares more for the things of the world than for God.

God created both you and the devil. He has all power over you and the devil. The devil owns nothing of what he is offering you. God owns all things in heaven and on the earth. The devil knows where he is headed, but God is giving you a chance at repentance, the salvation of your soul. "No one, having put his hand to the plow, and looking back, is fit for the kingdom of God" (Luke 9:62).

Has God not made it crystal clear to us in His Word as to the kind of lifestyle we must live if we want to see His face, the face of the Holy One? Have we ever stopped to count the cost of what it takes to follow Jesus? We cannot physically separate ourselves from the world, but we can separate ourselves morally and ethically by refusing to participate in the sinful lifestyle and evil practices of the world. Christians are in the world (physical presence) but not of this world (morally/spiritually separate). The road to salvation begins in Christ and ends in Christ. It is a straight and narrow path that must be followed by faith (continually trusting and believing in the Lord Jesus Christ). As one of the children from Faith, Love and Hope Ministry so eloquently put it, "You cannot take a shortcut to heaven."

Christians must make no assumptions about their own ability to persevere in faith to the end of this life. Our faith begins and ends with Christ. Christ is the author and finisher of our faith. We must trust in (stay with) Jesus every step of the way if we are to have any hope of completing this race, any hope of remaining on this road to salvation.

Salvation and Eternal Life

Here is the predicament of mankind. If a man continues in rebellion against God (refuses to believe in Jesus, refuses to repent), he is condemned. If he believes and follows Jesus halfheartedly, he is in danger of being disciplined by God. If he pretends to follow Jesus for a season or seasons in his life and then decides to turn back to a life of sin, he is without a doubt going to suffer wrath at the hands of God. The only way out of this predicament is Jesus Christ Himself. This is what I mean: Those who truly believe must submit to the Holy Spirit and let Him take total control of their lives—let Jesus reign as Lord—so that He can live through them and God's grace can work in them. They must hate their life, serve and follow Jesus (see John 12:25-26). Jesus knows the way. Jesus has made the way to heaven known to everyone who will receive it and believe it. He is the way to heaven. Jesus has been here and done that (except for sinning), and He made the T-shirt. He alone is qualified to take us through this journey to our salvation from beginning to end. The road to salvation is a journey with a beginning and an end, eternal life. Only in Jesus is there forgiveness of sin. If Jesus knew that Judas did not believe and would betray Him, He also knows those among us who are professors only (no heart change, no true repentance—those who are not in the faith.)

God is the God of the living. God told Moses that He is the God of Abraham, Isaac, and Jacob. He remains the same God today. Though each of these men died hundreds of years before Moses' encounter with God in the burning bush, they still live. Those who come to God must believe that He is. Abraham believed in the Lord, and God accounted it to him for righteousness (Genesis 15:6). God has relationship/ fellowship only with those who believe). Christians living a sinful lifestyle have no fellowship with God. They have not repented (let go) of sin, so therefore their sins remain. Those sins have not been forgiven.

There are seven words for peace between God and mankind. These words are the reality of a man's salvation after he comes to Christ through faith: Go your way

and sin no more. Salvation is a done deal for those who repent and follow Christ, for those who endure in belief. Jesus said, "You are from beneath; I am from above. You are of this world; I am not of this world. Therefore I said to you that you will die in your sins; for if you do not believe that I am He, you will die in your sins" (John 8:23-24).

The road to salvation is not marked by uncertainties. Repent and let Jesus forgive all of your sins. If Jesus forgives your sins then you will be saved, because His forgiveness is promised to all who trust in Him. If you keep your sins, then Jesus can do nothing for you. The evidence that you have inherited eternal life is God's Spirit given to those who believe. The evidence (the proof) to the world that you have the Holy Spirit will be the Christlike way that you live your life because it is Christ Himself—His life—that is in you. You cannot live as Christ without Christ.

One Man has the power to set everyone free who is held captive to sin in this world. Why would a person choose not to be set free? Every soul that rejects Christ after hearing the gospel has chosen to remain in bondage to sin. Who would turn down life (immortality)? Who would choose to die rather than to live? Countless people the world over are making the choice every day to turn down life by refusing to believe what the Bible says about Jesus Christ. Jesus offers His life. He gave His blood for their sins and they refuse it. **Sinners have a chance to see Jesus now through the eyes of faith and receive eternal life, or they can see Him later in judgment through eyes that have been condemned for all eternity because they refused His free gift of salvation.**

To reject Jesus Christ as your Lord and Savior is to reject God's only plan for the salvation of your soul. Jesus has already done the hard part. He has done all that was required. He shed His blood for our sins on the cross. He suffered the punishment of God for our sins. He died the death that should have been ours. He tasted death for everyone. There is nothing hard or difficult about receiving eternal life. It is a free gift from God. The difficulty many have is their reluctance to change—their unwillingness to let go of, or leave behind, the things of the world; to let go of the sinful pleasures the world offers them; to just believe what the Bible says.

The proof is in the pudding, as it is often said. The proof of your salvation is in the way you walk, talk, act, think, and do—the way you live your life each day. If your faith in Christ is genuine, it will manifest itself in your lifestyle daily. You will confess Christ as Lord and Savior before men and not be ashamed. As Jesus was not ashamed and confessed God as His Father before men, the true believer will also confess God as His Father and Jesus the Son of God as His Lord and Savior.

Those who have religion (absence of relationship with Christ) lay their religion down to practice sin, and when they are done they pick it up again. Some go behind closed doors and commit sinful acts (doing sinful things in secret as if the God they claim to know and serve is not omniscient [watching and listening, seeing all things]). Some do it in the open with no thought or regard for God. They disrespect Him before His enemies—not in darkness but in the light of day. On the other hand, those who have relationship with God through Jesus Christ know they are accountable for everything they do in the relationship so they walk circumspectly, not as fools but as wise. Wisdom is the principal thing, therefore get wisdom. Wisdom leads the believer to make choices that are in keeping with God's purposes and desires.

Do not be deceived, professing Christian. You cannot serve God when you choose and how you choose—in your own way with earthly wisdom—and conclude that eternal life is yours. Perhaps you simply have not settled the question, "What shall I do with Jesus?" Do I believe in Him or not? Do I follow Him or not? Do I love Him or not? Do I make Him Lord of my life? Until you settle this important matter you will continue in sin.

"And this is eternal life, that they may know You, the only true God, and Jesus Christ whom You have sent" (John 17:3). Eternal life is a never-ending relationship with the Father and the Son that begins on earth in regeneration. Eternal life is the result of what Jesus did on the cross. Jesus came so that we may have life and life more abundantly. A Christian must never forget that he is a sinner saved by grace. As long as the sin nature exists, he will sin against God. He will commit sin as an exception because of his sinful nature that he chooses to yield to and because his flesh is weak. But he will not wallow in sin, practicing it on a continual basis. Therefore, he is in daily need of God's forgiveness in order to remain in fellowship with Him..

After we are converted from unsaved sinner to saved sinner, we must be washed/cleansed daily of the sins we commit against God (see 1 John 1:9). If we confess our sins daily, then Jesus Christ, who is our Advocate with the Father, pleads on our behalf in order that we might retain fellowship with God. If Jesus does not wash us, we fall out of fellowship with God (John 13:1-11). We all sin, day in and day out, every one of us. If we say we have not sinned, then we call God a liar. We show that His Word has no place in our hearts. The daily confession and forgiveness of our sins is essential to maintaining our fellowship with God.

Is your eternity with God secure? Are you sure? If you do not live by and obey God's Word on earth, you will not do it in heaven. If you do not love God now, you will not love God in heaven. This is the time of preparation. In order to be prepared for Christ's return, we must live God's way today, tomorrow, and each and every day. We must live a consistent life of obedience unto God. In doing so we can be confident that Christ's return will not take us by surprise. For if the righteous one is scarcely saved, where will the ungodly and the sinner appear? (1 Peter 4:18). It is a terrible thing to know what is required and not do it. We must take the first step down here to get it right in Christ. We cannot wait until we get to heaven. We make things right with God now. God brings perfection later. Jesus Christ is coming soon. Blessed are those who obey God's Word, who keep His commandments. Will Christ find you prepared when He returns?

Imagine having sand in one hand and a rock in the other. Which of the two can you hold onto? The rock, correct? Jesus is the Rock, the eternal Son of God. If you hold onto Him, you gain eternal life. "For you have need of endurance, so that after you have done the will of God, you may receive the promise: For yet a little while, and He who is coming will come and will not tarry. Now the just shall live by faith; but if anyone draws back, My soul has no pleasure in him. But we are not of those who draw back to perdition, but of those who believe to the saving of the soul" (Hebrews 10:36-39). The end of our faith is the salvation of our soul (see 1 Peter 1:3-12).

Happy (blessed) are those who are strong in the Lord, who set their minds on a pilgrimage (Psalm 84:5). We must set (be deliberate; not changing; steadfast) our minds on God, on heaven; we must set our minds on doing what is right and pleasing unto God. It is a pilgrimage to heaven. Jesus set His face steadfast toward Jerusalem because He was intent on doing what He had come to do. He was determined that no one or nothing would take Him off course. We too must set our faces steadfast toward heaven if we are intent on living the life God has called us to live.

The Decision

For those who profess Christ but are still living in sin, I implore you to let it go. What do you gain other than temporary earthly pleasure and fleeting happiness? You separate yourself from God. You forsake the Lord, the fountain of living water. Therefore, do not boast about being spiritual as a Christian when you live in sin. It is a fearful thing to fall into the hands of the living God. Can you not see the flashing red light warning you of the danger that lies ahead? If you practice saying no to the devil (making it a habitual lifestyle), you will eventually realize the power you have in Christ over the sinful nature. How did Jesus say no to Satan when he tempted Him in the wilderness? Jesus' response was always, "It is written." There is no greater power on earth among believers than that which resides in the heart of a believer. It is the Word of God, the Word of God's power. We hide God's word in our hearts so that we might not sin against Him—in order to have the power to resist temptation..

He who sins is of the devil (1 John 3:8). A sinning Christian allows the devil to use him (to make a fool of him) by giving in to the temptations, and God watches it all from His throne in heaven. Some have sinned for so long that what they do seems right. Sin is no longer ugly in their sight. They sin without remorse. They are just another link in the devil's chain of fools. They are a slave of the devil because it is his voice that they obey. Jesus came to redeem the world from slavery to sin. What has happened to them to cause them to do what they are doing? Have they grown tired of God? Have they grown tired of waiting for Jesus to return, waiting for the promise? Have they grown weary in doing good?

The Bible tells us that Jesus will lose none that the Father has given Him. For whom the Lord loves He chastens (disciplines). "But if you are without chastening, of which all have become partakers, then you are illegitimate and not sons" (Hebrews 12:3-8). You must be absolutely sure that you belong to Christ. Whoever has been born of God does not sin, for His seed remains in Him, and he cannot sin because he has been born of God. If you profess that you are a Christian yet you are not compelled to live as Jesus lived (according to the Word of God) then perhaps you need to question whether or not you have received the Holy Spirit of God, whether or not you have been born again. Habitual sin is not consistent with the Christian lifestyle. "The Lord knows those who are His," and, "Let everyone who names the name of Christ depart from iniquity" (2 Timothy 2:19). Darkness and light cannot coexist, because when the light shines (is turned on) the darkness has to flee. I encourage you to live your life based on the truth of God's Word. One day you will die but you don't know when. One day Jesus will return but you don't know when. Those who die in their sins die as an enemy of God, and when Jesus comes back He will not come back for the enemies of God. If you die as an enemy of God, you will forever remain an enemy of God. The truth never changes.

More important than knowing the truth is believing the truth. **The evidence that a person believes Jesus' words is when you see that person living according to Jesus' words.** No man or woman can be a true follower of Jesus Christ and their lives remain the same. The power of Jesus transforms. It makes the old new, the unclean clean, the unrighteous righteous, the unholy holy. It makes the sinner a saint! The power of Jesus will make the believer hate sin. If there has been no change as far as sin is concerned in a professing Christian's life, he should check to make sure he is plugged into the Power Source. If he learns by conviction of the Holy Spirit that he is not, then he should come to Christ and let Him circumcise his heart. He should then lay aside every weight and the sin that so easily ensnares him. He should finally run with endurance the race that is set before him, looking unto Jesus, the author and finisher of his faith.

Make the decision today to surrender completely to Jesus and follow Him home to the place that has been prepared for those who love and obey God. A Christian will know if his/her heart is surrendered to God when he/she allows nothing or no one to come before God and His kingdom business. God's will is the highest priority in his life. As it was for Jesus, so shall it be for those who follow Him.

Turn from sin and live. Sin leads to death. Obedience leads to life. If you sincerely practice being obedient to Christ today—sincerely try to do your best to please God in the power of God's Spirit—then you can sincerely practice obedience every day. You must make it a habit of practicing righteousness. It is a matter of surrendering your will. Blessed are those who hunger and thirst after righteousness. God will fill them.

God takes no pleasure in the death of the wicked. God desires that no man perish but that all come to repentance. If you are thinking along the lines as some people do that a good God surely will not send a man to hell because he has done some good in his life, it is evidence against you that you really do not know the true and living God. It is evidence that you do not understand sin—what it is, what it did in the beginning, and what it continues doing now in the lives of those whom God has created in His image, according to His likeness. You do not understand the nature of sin and what sin is doing in the world. As a result of sin, God has to redeem all things—man, the earth, everything—in order to get rid of sin.

Any good works that a man does that are not done for Jesus Christ, in His name, will not remain when his works are judged by God. Why? The answer is simple: the good was done for self. It was done to bring him satisfaction, to make him feel good and look good in the eyes of man. It was not done out of love for Christ. Only what a man does for Christ has any eternal value. A man's works must be done in keeping with repentance and with the right motive in order to last. Although someone benefited from the good that he did, it was not done in Jesus' name. It was not done to bring God glory. God prepared the works and God created man and prepared him for the works. If a man is not doing what God has prepared, then his works are not for the glory of God. The bottom line is this: If your name is not found among the ones written in the Book of Life, then you leave God no choice but to judge you guilty and cast you into the lake of fire on the day of the great white throne judgment (Revelation 20:11-15).

The God of heaven, who is gracious and compassionate, perfect in His love for all mankind—the God who gives life (eternal life) to all who believe in Jesus—is the same God who is perfect and just in His wrath and judgment of sin. He will take a man's life, the same man that He offers eternal life to and who refuses it, and cast his soul into hell for sins against Him.

All that really matters in this life is preparation for the next. A man must prepare his soul either to live with God or to live without God. Decide today to come to Jesus Christ and live.

Good Works That Glorify God

For those who have already given up all rights to self and are wholeheartedly following Jesus (those who sin less, have stopped living the sinful lifestyle), I encourage you to help those brothers and sisters who are weak in the faith so that they too may grow strong and become vessels God can use. Pray for all who come and are now in Christ that their faith will not fail. Encourage and motivate those whom you see sinning against God to repent and return to Christ. Correct and rebuke in love and kindness. Do all that you can with the help of the Lord.

Do not be a silent Christian, keeping the Good News shut up inside. God has committed to you, Christ's ambassador, the Word of reconciliation. Share the Word in love and kindness with those who are lost and on their way to hell, those who do not realize or understand that God does not like ugly. God's eternal plan of salvation in the message of the cross is foolishness to those who are perishing, but to us who are being saved it is the power of God. For since, in the wisdom of God, the world through wisdom did not know God, it pleased God through the foolishness of the message preached to save those who believe. The foolishness of God is wiser than men and the weakness of God is stronger than men (1 Corinthians 1:18-25).

Do not be a closet Christian—going out to church on Sundays only and then hiding yourself Monday through Saturday. Let your light shine so people may see your good works and glorify your Father in heaven.

Be encouraged and do not be afraid to take a stand for the truth (to tell the truth). If someone gets angry because you tell the truth, tell it anyway. Plant the seed of life and let God do the rest. Let God by His Spirit lead that soul to Christ.

Finally, make God look good in the life you live down here. Live a godly life in Christ for God. God has chosen you to represent Him, His holy name. He has entrusted His Word to you. He has given you the great honor and privilege of winning souls for His kingdom. He will one day reward you with the promise to see Him and spend eternity with Him. What other motivation do we need in order to serve God, follow Christ, and obey the Holy Spirit while here on earth than the promise to see His face and to hear Him say, "Well done, My good and faithful servant"?

CHAPTER 5

WHERE ARE THE LABORERS?

Moses was eighty years old when God told him:

> Come now, therefore, and I will send you
> to Pharaoh that you may bring My people,
> the children of Israel, out of Egypt (Exodus
> 3:10).

God promised Moses that He would certainly be with him. Let us fast forward to the first century. The eleven disciples met Jesus as instructed on the mountain in Galilee. It was there that Jesus gave them what we refer to today as the Great Commission. Jesus promised to be with them always even until the end of the age.

After more than two thousand years, God is still speaking to us through His holy Word. Like God, the Word of God never changes. God is with us. Let those who have ears to hear, hear what the Word has to say about the responsibility—the Christian duty—of those who believe in Christ to labor in the fields. There are, I believe, many people who believe in Christ but have not become His disciples.

God has not given us the option to choose whether or not we want to do what He commands. We disobey Him when we do not do what He says, and our disobedience will have its reward. We must remember that it is almighty God we have entered into a covenant relationship with through His Son Jesus Christ.

Since entering the covenant, have you been faithful? Have you sincerely been living for Christ, doing His will? Or have you been preoccupied with self and the things of this world so much so that you are of little use to God? God cannot put you in a dark place and let you be the light. God cannot send you because of weak faith; you do not know the Scriptures or the power of God. If the entire world were saved, there would be no work for Christians to do. As long as there is one soul not saved, we have work to do. So many people are weary and scattered, like sheep without a shepherd. Much work remains to be done for the kingdom of God. The harvest is so great but the workers are few (Luke 10:2).

The work of harvesting lost souls—laboring in the fields of the Lord—is not for those who are weak in faith, lazy, lukewarm, or lovers of the world. They stand by gazing up into the sky, watching yet not working while waiting for the Savior's return, making light of the work that has to be done. The command was to go and make disciples. Have you been made a disciple of Jesus? To make one a disciple means *to prepare, to anoint, to be changed into; to produce as a result of action, effort or behavior.* A disciple of Jesus is one who follows Him through His teachings. A disciple of Jesus is an imitator of Him and His way of life. A disciple of Jesus is a servant. Are you following His teaching, abiding in His Word, imitating His way of life?

The cost to be a disciple of Jesus is great. To be Jesus' disciple means no longer living and thinking like people who do not know Jesus or who do not believe that a day of judgment is on the way. It means a life of moral living versus immoral living, no longer indulging the flesh by giving in to its sinful desires. Jesus gave His body for the Father's use (see Romans 8:3 NLT). A disciple of Jesus sacrifices his body to show that he has stopped sinning, and by doing so he too can be used by the Father. Self-control of the members of one's body is paramount in following Christ.

Hell—Real or Not
"But know this, that in the last days perilous times will come: For men will be lovers of themselves, lovers of money, boasters, proud, blasphemers, disobedient to parents, unthankful, unholy, unloving, unforgiving, slanderers, without self-control, brutal, despisers of good, traitors, headstrong, haughty, lovers of pleasure rather than lovers of God, having a form of godliness but denying its power" (2 Timothy 3:1-5). This reads like the news reports/stories we are bombarded with day after day by the media. Does anyone besides Jesus Christ have any good news to tell? Which of you truly believes that we are in the last days? If you say you believe, what are you doing about it? What are you doing in order to bring more souls into the kingdom of God?

Do you ever think about hell (the lake of fire)? Do you truly believe that hell is a real place as told to us in the Word of God and that once a soul goes there it shall never have rest but will be tormented forever (Revelation 14:11)? Or is it just science fiction, some figment of our imagination, and people are living in hell right here on earth as some have said? The suffering of a man here on earth will be inconsequential compared to the eternal separation from God that he will suffer when he is judged guilty of sin. Eternal separation from God in hell is forever as eternal life with Christ in heaven is forever. Jesus tried to get the people to see this in

Luke 13:2-5. They thought that violent and tragic death was a result of great sin. The conclusion Jesus wanted the people to reach was that all sinners, unless they repent, will perish (live spiritually separated from God forever).

When you envision hell, what do you see? What images, if any, come to mind? What are your thoughts concerning the place? What is it that you contemplate as you think about the souls that shall end up there? If you have read God's Word concerning the matter and you believe what you have read, then you know that it is a place you certainly do not want to go. In turn, do you picture hell as a place where you would not want the soul of any person to be destroyed (not annihilation but ruination) by God? God commands us in Matthew 10:28 to love our neighbor as ourselves. Who is our neighbor?

Perhaps you try not to think about hell at all. The very thought makes you uncomfortable, uneasy. By not thinking about it you have failed to allow yourself to be transformed by the renewing of your mind. When your mind is renewed, you see things as God sees things. **You see as Jesus did when He said, "The harvest truly is plentiful, but the laborers are few. Therefore, pray the Lord of the harvest to send out laborers into His harvest"** (Matthew 9:37). With a renewed mind you understand why Jesus was moved with compassion when He saw the multitudes weary and scattered, like sheep having no shepherd. With a renewed mind you fully understand the urgency, the necessity, of working now while you still have light, while you still have breath in your body. People may honestly have no concept of the resurrection of Jesus. People may honestly have no concept that death without repentance is forever. People may honestly have no concept of the blackest darkness—that death is not the absence of life but rather the absence of the Light, the Lord Jesus Christ. Psalm 49:19 tells us that the wicked will never again see the light of day. Spiritual death is the absence of God forever in the lives of those who refuse to believe in Jesus.

People may honestly have no concept of God's coming judgment. A person will only set things right with God in this life if he believes God is going to judge him in the next (2 Timothy 4:1). **A man who will not believe in Jesus is one breath away from spiritual death forever. If a man dies and carries his sins with him to the grave, there is nothing anyone can do for him—not even the Lord Jesus Christ. It is too late for repentance...too late for his salvation.** If he does not go down to the grave justified by God (in right standing/right relationship with God), he will be judged guilty of sin against God. When his body is resurrected from the dead, he will stand before God and receive his sentence of eternal damnation. This is why believers all over the world must share the gospel with the utmost urgency. They must tell the lost about Jesus Christ. The call to repentance and salvation goes forth by the Word of God. Each time someone with an unrepentant heart hears the gospel, it is a divine summons to repent and confess sins in order to be forgiven and saved. Believers must tell the world who Jesus is and why they must believe in Him. The planting and watering of Christ's seed (the Word of God) must be done so that God will give the increase.

To Serve or Not to Serve

Wherever you are right now, you are standing in the fields of God. Perhaps in your neighborhood, your own household, at work, the supermarket, gas station, the park, the battlefield, on a tropical island relaxing and enjoying a vacation/retirement, and yes, sadly, even in the church there are souls who are lost and in need of harvesting. Some professing Christians lack understanding concerning the church (the universal body of Christ as opposed to the physical building). When a person believes in the name of

Jesus and accepts Jesus as his personal Lord and Savior, he becomes a member of the body of Christ—the church for which Christ will return. The Bible makes it clear that a man is saved by God's grace through faith. He who believes in the Son has everlasting life; and he who does not believe the Son shall not see life, but the wrath of God abides on him (John 3:36). Coming out, whether regularly or on occasion, and sitting inside a building on Sundays does not make a person a Christian. It does not save anyone's soul. A man is not saved by works. If a man believes he is saved because he goes to church, he believes a lie and is worse off than the man who has never heard the gospel.

Christians must be ever so careful to let no one's damnation be attributed to their account (Acts 20:26). It is not for Christians to pick and choose to whom they will witness (share the gospel with). We are still flawed human beings in the flesh even though we have God's Spirit indwelling us. God in His wisdom knew that we would need His help. That is why God gave us His Spirit, the Helper. We must be led by the Spirit of God. The Spirit of God sees a lost soul (a rebellious heart against God; someone in need of salvation), and that is all we should see through the eyes of Christ. The fields of God are ripe for harvest, containing crops (souls) that are rich, poor, male, female, educated, uneducated, general officers and privates, old and young, people of every nation and every tongue. The fields contain crops of sinners that need to be saved (harvested). The family of God will come from people of every race and nation and every walk of life.

What happens if a farmer fails to harvest his crop? The crop dies and the farmer will suffer loss. A Christian who is unfaithful and disobedient in this matter of soul harvesting will also suffer loss—missed blessings now and rewards later. Mordecai sent a message to Queen Esther that if she remained completely silent at that time, relief and deliverance would arise. Yet who knew whether she had come to the kingdom for such a time? God has put you where you are not to remain silent, but to bring relief and deliverance to those who need it. But because you are *not* doing what you should be doing, God has to send somebody else.

What happens to the crop after it is planted and watered? It produces a harvest. God controls how abundant the harvest is, not the farmer. It is the same with harvesting lost souls. Someone plants and another waters, but God gives the increase. Someone reaps that which another has sown, and they both rejoice together. You may never see or know what God has done with the seeds of His Word that were planted by you in the heart of an unbeliever here on earth. But if you make it to heaven I believe you will see the fruit gathered for eternal life as a result of your labors (John 4:27-38).

Go out into the Lord's harvest in the wisdom and power of the Holy Spirit, doubting nothing. Do not get discouraged if people reject you, for it is not you they reject but Christ. Do not think that your labor is in vain; just keep telling folks the Good News. If you do not go out and witness as though you truly believe what you are telling other people about Jesus, then your witness will be less effective. Doubt negatively impacts witnessing. The unbelievers who are in frequent contact with you ought to see with their own eyes just how powerful Christ is because your life ought to be and continues to be transformed. Your character ought to become more and more like Christ. Unbelievers ought to see some visible evidence that the invisible God you serve is with you (Exodus 33:12-17). They should see His life-changing power at work in your life. Is your faith in God known by those within your sphere of influence? Can you honestly say that your life is a surrendered life, a reflection of the holiness of God? God will work in and through you when you become a humble servant.

Ask yourself this question and truthfully answer it. Is my heart right with God? If you are trying to serve two masters, then God cannot use you to represent Him. You have not made the choice between the two masters. This indecisiveness renders you combat ineffective as a soldier in the army of the Lord. Your lifestyle testifies *against* you instead of testifying *for* Christ that He lives inside your heart. You have got to get yourself together with the help of the Lord. You have to start living the way God wants you to live. When you begin to live by His Word, God by His grace will produce abundant results. It is the Lord's harvest. You are the Lord's servant.

Professing Christian, do not let this charge be brought against you. Someone asks, "What must I do to be saved?" and for lack of knowledge about your own faith, you cannot give him the answer because you have not studied the Bible in order to show yourself approved. You are not committed and devoted to the Word of truth. Knowledge of the Scriptures is paramount in winning souls for the kingdom of God. Christians must know the Scriptures (the doctrines of Christ).

We are told in Acts 8:35 that when the eunuch asked Philip about whom the prophet was speaking, Philip opened his mouth and preached Jesus to Him. To be ignorant of the Scriptures, lacking knowledge and understanding of Jesus Christ, is a terrible thing for a professing Christian. If a Christian does not know the Scriptures, how can he tell an unsaved soul about the things above, about the One who came down from heaven and has returned there, and that those who believe in Him will one day be with Him? It is a sad commentary of the life he has been living. What in this life is that Christian doing if not preparing for the next one in heaven? It is God's Word that should fill our hearts and our minds. It is His Word that should lie hidden in our hearts so that we might not sin against Him. It is His Word that we should speak—the Word of Truth—for it will last forever.

What is your attitude toward sin? Toward sinners? Are you indifferent (lukewarm)—it matters not to you one way or the other? Does it bother you that people are living apart from God now because of sin and if they continue in it until death and do not repent, you know they will live apart from Him forever? Television networks sometimes air programs where someone has been reconciled with a loved one after many years of separation. If the secular world will go to great lengths to reconnect (reunite, reconcile) loved ones, why can't Christians do the same? Why can't we go to great lengths at any cost, enduring trials/suffering/tribulation, give and do whatever it takes to reconcile God's children to Him? We can do it with the help, wisdom, and power of God. The real issue is will we do it? It really boils down to whether or not we believe this endeavor of soul harvesting is worth the sacrifice of our time, money, gifts, and ourselves. God's grace is what brought us to Him. It is this same grace that will bring the others back to Him (2 Corinthians 4:15).

The multitudes all over the world that are aimlessly and hopelessly wandering the earth need to know. They need to hear that Jesus loves them. It is unlikely that God is going to come down and speak to them from the mountaintop. He has given those who believe His Word and His Spirit. He will speak to the lost through the mouths of those who believe. We do not have the power to save one soul, but we do have a mouth and the ability to communicate the Word of God; the Holy Spirit by His power will bring conviction to the heart that hears the truth. If you are not willing to tell someone the truth, at least invite him out to church so someone else can tell him. He will enter the church and hear Christ preached, the truth, and when he believes the truth he will be saved. He will receive God's Spirit to seal him as God's own. Not by might nor by power but by My Spirit says the Lord (Zechariah 4:6).

The farmer looks out over the fields as far as his eyes can see when it is harvesttime. He sees how great the harvest is. He sees how God has blessed the work of his hands. Can you not see the great harvest in the fields of the Lord? So many souls are lost. So many souls are being lied to and deceived. Many are giving in to any and every wind of doctrine in their search for the truth. Why? Because man has distorted the truth of God's Word in order to draw a following (Acts 20:30).

Some of you were probably not aware of this responsibility that you inherited—to go out and labor in the fields of the Lord. It goes back to that count-the-cost conversation our Lord Jesus had with some folks more than two thousand years ago. It goes back to James's words on faith without works being dead. It goes back to the Great Commission that Jesus gave His disciples more than two thousand years ago. He made known the will of God (the mind of God) concerning the matter of how God will use believers to further the kingdom. "All authority has been given to Me in heaven and on earth. Go therefore and make disciples of all the nations, baptizing them in the name of the Father and of the Son and of the Holy Spirit, teaching them to observe all things that I have commanded you; and lo, I am with you always, even until the end of the age" (Matthew 28:18-20).

Did you read anywhere in those verses that Jesus said go when your life is in perfect order, go when you have received complete knowledge and understanding of His Word, go when your finances are in order, go when you have the right house, go when you have served Him for a certain number of years, go when you retire from your job, go when the weather is right, go when there is peace and no war, go only where the people are of your same race and ethnicity, etc.? No, you did not, so what is preventing you from following the Lord's command? If it was due to ignorance (you simply did not know), that no longer remains an obstacle. Now that you are aware of your responsibility, what will you do with this revelation, this knowledge? Faith, like Isaiah had, says, "Here am I! Send me." Faith, like Jesus at the age of twelve, says, "I must be about my Father's business." Do you have this kind of faith? If not, do you desire to have it? Ask God and He will give it to you.

On the other hand there are those who know and have known for quite some time about this responsibility (the Father's business) but have simply lived to please them-selves rather than God. I believe this falls under the sin of disobedience. You may have asked, "What is in it for me to labor in the fields?" Ask yourself, "What does God owe me?" Answer: Absolutely nothing! Ask yourself, "What do I owe God?" Answer: A debt you can never repay. You labor out of love, not expecting anything in return. You do it out of obedience to please God. You do it *For God's Glory.*

Life on earth for believers is about dying and living. Dying to self and living for Christ. The world has it back-wards. The world says life is about living—getting all you can and doing all you can; enjoying what this life has to offer while you can. Why? Because the world's attitude is that it is their thing and it is their stuff and they can do what they want to do with it and no God in heaven can tell them otherwise. The world believes that when you are dead you are done. And the world does not know God. The unbeliever sees death as the end of all things. Little does he realize that death is only the end of his physical life here on earth. His earthly body will return to the dust, but his soul will live forever. But you, O child of God, know that death is the beginning of eternal blessedness in the presence of the Savior for those who believe, or the beginning of a terrible life of damnation, torment, and eternal ruin (eternal separa-tion from God) forever for the unbeliever, the unrepentant soul (Luke 16:19-31).

For those currently not counted among the laborers, ask yourself, "What more must Jesus do for me to love Him as He deserves, for me to walk away from the sinful pleasures of the world and dedicate my life to faithfully serving Him? What more must Jesus do for me to become a laborer?" There is nothing more that He will do. He has suffered the punishment for your sins—the punishment of death. He has suffered at the hands of those who hated Him without a cause—those who beat Him mercilessly, spit on Him, mocked Him, treated Him harshly, and then crucified Him. He has given you His Word that He will be with you always. He has given you His Spirit as a guarantee of your inheritance and to empower you for the work in the fields. He grants you new mercies each day. He is providing for your every need each day. He has given you life—eternal life. All God wants is for you to give your time, your gifts, your money, your talent, but most of all yourself. The Bible tells us that it is more blessed to give than to receive. We ought to give back to God all that He has given us for His glory here on earth. All that we have can be used by Him in our service to Him down here.

Are you willing to let God use you so that people may come to know and believe in Him and see His works? Are you willing to take your place among those who are laborers for Christ?

A Time for All Things

Woe to those who find themselves as goats and not sheep, as tares and not wheat, as enemies of God and not friends of God on judgment day. Do you know why God gave the land flowing with milk and honey, the rich and fertile land of Canaan to the children of Israel? It was not because they deserved it or had done anything to earn it (again God owes no man anything). It was because of the promise He made to Abraham. It was because the inhabitants had defiled the land. Their iniquity was complete so God removed them from the land. The land belonged to God. He took it away and gave it to the children of Israel (see Genesis 15). Surely you understand that this earth and everything in it belongs to God. God owns all things. They are His to do with as He pleases. One day the iniquity of all mankind will be complete.

God created each and every human being. God loves each and every human being. Yes, even those who are the most evil and wicked in the eyes of man (John 3:16). God has determined a time for each and every human being to live and to die. The final outcome of all events rests in His hands. As a Christian do not look at death through the eyes of the world. Look at it through the eyes of Christ. Start seeing mankind as God sees mankind. We know that death comes to everyone because of sin and that God takes no pleasure in the death of the wicked. We know because the Bible tells us so. The Word of God reveals how messed up we creatures of the dust (human beings) really are (see Romans 3:10-18). The Word of God reveals how great is the need for change in everyone's heart. **Heart surgery by man prolongs life. Circumcision of the heart by Christ gives life, eternal life. Is there someone you know who is in need of a new heart today?**

Yes, God is a good God. God is merciful, but He is also holy, righteous, and just. The sin of unbelief will be judged, and those found guilty will be punished. God will one day remove all sin forever. All who refuse God's free gift of salvation—all whose sins remain—will be judged and sentenced to hell forever. They will not get a second chance to accept Christ. There will be no parole boards where they go. They will not get time off for "good behavior." They will never cross the great gulf that separates them from the believers. Are you beginning to see things down here as God sees things from up there?

Do not attempt to reason with God in the matter saying there is some good in everyone and surely God will consider this. God's ways and God's thoughts are not like ours. God will judge everyone according to the things done in the body. Jesus said, "Repent." Jesus meant repent. Jesus came the first time to save that which was lost. Now is the time for everyone to stop sinning and obey God. Jesus will come again to bring judgment. There is no gray area in this matter with God. A man either believes what the Bible teaches or he does not. And if he believes, it is God's message of salvation and judgment that should go forth from his mouth at every opportunity. Jonah preached a message of judgment from God. Every sinner needs to hear this same message today. A day is coming when God will judge their sins. Jesus stands ready to forgive their sins in order that they might escape this judgment.

Jesus came and died for the sins of the world. Everyone who hears the gospel has an opportunity to repent (turn from sin and follow Christ). Paul writes in Romans 10:14, "How shall they believe in Him of whom they have not heard?" Herein lies the importance of your obedience in taking your place among the laborers. **An unbeliever will not know whether or not he believes in Jesus until he hears the Good News, the gospel of his salvation.** Those who refuse to believe after they have heard have refused their only hope for salvation.

We must present the gospel and give people the option to choose (accept or reject) Christ, to obey God or continue in disobedience as Joshua did thousands of years ago (Joshua 24:14-15). People need to know that a better day is coming and they can be included. They can share in it when it does come (Revelation 21:1-4; 22:1-5). People also need to know that a day of judgment is coming and only those who believe in Jesus will escape and enter the New Jerusalem (Revelation 21:27).

Christians should grieve as they see and hear the accounts of all that is going on in the world and the countless thousands who are dying each day without Christ. The Bible tells us that hell enlarges itself daily. Christians ought to pray that the Lord will send out laborers. Christians ought to pray that God will teach them and send them out as one of the laborers. Christians ought to pray that the gospel will go forth unhindered to every ear and every nation so that people will hear the truth and repent, accept Christ as their Lord and Savior, and enter into eternal life.

Christians ought to speak with one voice the message that Christ taught in order for a person to be saved (Matthew 4:17; 18:3; John 3:3,16-18; 5:24; 6:47-48 ; Acts 16:29-33). Paul told Timothy to preach the Word. What Word? The Word Timothy received from Paul. The Word Paul received from the Lord Jesus Christ. The Word Jesus received from the Father (John 12:49-50). Every Christian's message must be the same regarding the salvation of a man's soul—if he believes on the Lord Jesus Christ he will be saved. We should add nothing to the message or take nothing away from the message but speak the truth in love as it is written (Deuteronomy 4:2; Revelation 22:18-19). It is this truth that sets a person free. *The Word of God (the Bible) has been clearly telling people for over two thousand years that Jesus is the Christ—the Savior of the world—yet countless numbers will not believe.*

Have you taken notice of the oneness of God concerning the things of God? Jesus said, "I and My Father are one" (John 10:30). Christ has made both Jew and Gentile one (Ephesians 2:14). Christ created in Himself one new man from the two that He might reconcile them both to God in one body through the cross (Ephesians 2:15-16). Through Christ both have access by one Spirit to the Father (Ephesians 2:18). There is one Lord, one faith, one baptism; one God and Father of all.

Therefore, since there is only one eternal kingdom of God, should we not conclude then that there should be only one message, one way as to how one may enter it? Contrary to the belief of some, all religions do not lead to the true and living God. Why would God give Jesus His Son one message as to how a man must be saved and give a different message to earthly men? Jesus is from above. Men are of this world. God would not and He did not. *I implore you not to base your salvation, your hope for eternal life, on what men say but rather on what the Bible says. What does God say you must do in order to be saved? God knows, it is His heaven, listen to Him.*

Do not be ashamed of the gospel of Jesus Christ. It is the power of God at work, saving everyone who believes. God makes people right with Himself through faith (Romans 5:1-2). The difference between Jesus Christ and religion is the difference between eternal life or eternal damnation. Many people the world over have religion, but few in comparison have Jesus as their Lord and Savior. The time for Christians to tell people the truth and stand by it is now.

Love the Lord Thy God

Love means sacrifice. Those who love God must sacrifice their life down here so that others may come to know the love Jesus has for the world. Jesus died that we might live. We must die to self in order for Christ to live in us and for the power of God to work in and through us. We are told by Paul to present our bodies as a living sacrifice. God's measuring stick for love for Him is sacrifice. Our sacrifice is the measure of our love for God. If we are not devoted and committed to God, the things of God, the Word of God—if we are not preoccupied with God—if we are faithless and unfaithful, then God cannot use us.

When we tell God we love Him, we are in essence saying, I am obeying Your Word, I am keeping Your commandments, I am living how Your Word says I ought to live. "Not my will but Thy will be done" says, "I love

You, Lord." To love is to act. Love is an action word! Talk is cheap; words without action mean nothing. God told the children of Israel that all day long they honored Him with their mouths but their hearts were far from Him. They were too busy living for themselves—doing what they wanted to do—to be concerned about the things of God, the ways of God, and the commands of God. So it is with some Christians. We are too preoccupied with the world and the things of the world, things that are going to pass away, and as a result our relationship with Jesus suffers. Yet we say to Him, "Lord, I love You."

Where is our sacrifice? Greater love has no one than to lay down his life for a friend. Aren't believers friends of Jesus? God is love. It is His natural attribute. Love for God will lead us to a love for lost souls.

When we allow the Holy Spirit to transform our character to that of Jesus Christ, we too will love others as Christ loved us. When we begin to see from God's view, we realize that it isn't about us at all—our health, our wealth, how big the house, how luxurious the car, what job title and professional degrees we hold, what wonders of the world we can jet off to see before we leave this earth. It's about harvesting souls.

Those who are well do not need a doctor; only those who are sick need a doctor. Jesus taught what He knew, what He had seen and heard, what He was told by the Father in heaven (John 3:31b-32a). He knew that God created hell for Satan and his angels, and the people who sin against God without repentance will also go to hell. If we would simply see with our spiritual eyes what awaits those who are going to be judged guilty by God, we would understand why Jesus came and died and why God has kept us here after He sealed us as His own. It is so He can work in us (preparing us for eternity; sanctification) and through us (gathering together the other family members from every nation; reconciliation). Can the

Lord send you out and count on you to be a faithful laborer? Will you go for Him simply because you love Him?

Heavenly Father, I pray that You will give Your children great power to give witness to the resurrection of the Lord Jesus. Open to them a door for the Word, to speak the mystery of Christ. Pour out Your grace upon them all. In Jesus name I pray. Amen.

CHAPTER 6

SPIRITUAL CHECK-UP:
HOW'S YOUR WALK
BY FAITH?

Grace: God's love for sinful and helpless mankind (His creation) in action. He sent His Son to die for our sins.

Faith: Man's love for God in action. We obey God's Word because our sins have been forgiven.

In his book *Heaven or Hell*, R.A. Torrey tells the story of a woman who was dying and called for the minister of her church to come to her home. When he arrived she told him she had been a professing Christian for forty years. She told him she was now dying and found out that she was never saved at all.

For forty years this woman professed Christ as her Savior, but now as she lay dying, she realized she never had faith (trusted/believed) in Jesus Christ after all. I fear that many professing Christians today may be in this same condition.

They have never received a new heart from God, nor has God renewed a right spirit within them. They go to church (often/ sometime/rarely, if ever)—a man-made building—but they are not a member of the church, the body of Christ. They are not counted among the children of God. Why? Because they do not believe in Jesus. Their trust is not in Him and Him alone to save them. **A strong indicator that a man is trying to get to heaven by works instead of faith alone in Christ is when he does something in order to receive something in return from God. He expects God to do something for him (reward him with eternal life) because he has done something for God. God owes no man that He should have to repay him. Salvation is a free gift from God that is offered to everyone. But it will only be received by those who believe in Jesus Christ.**

When God gave the law through Moses to the Israelites on Mount Sinai, it was a sign of the covenant. By obedience, the children of Israel would continue to be God's covenant people. We learn from God's Word that they did not obey God. They constantly sinned/rebelled against Him. Because of unbelief they disobeyed, they broke the covenant and forfeited their right to be the chosen people. Because of the children of Israel's sin, salvation has come to the Gentiles (see Isaiah 56 for salvation for the Gentiles).

Today, the cross of Cavalry is a sign of the covenant. A person enters into a covenant with God when he hears the gospel (the Word of truth); believes that the life, death, and resurrection of Jesus really happened (Ephesians 1:13; Mark 15:33-16:7); believes that these events are indisputable historical facts; believes (trusts) what the Bible says about Jesus—that He is the Son of God, the Savior of the world (1 John 4:14); and that He saves all who repent and come to Him for forgiveness of their sins.

By truly believing the gospel, that Jesus is the Christ, the Son of God, you are born again. That faith entitles you to the power of God—the power that will save your soul. You are reconciled to God, no longer alienated, and immediately ushered into a personal relationship with God through Christ. This relationship comes as a result of a change of the unbelieving heart—a change of attitude toward sin that God sees in a sinner's heart. Jesus explained to Nicodemus in John 3 that he (Nicodemus) couldn't explain how people are born again (of the Spirit). No one can explain this new birth today any more than Nicodemus could, but the true believer gives witness that his spirit has been regenerated. He has been born again; he has new life. The presence of the Holy Spirit demonstrates the genuineness of a believer's faith. His change in lifestyle from living as the world lives to how Christ says he ought to live is his testimony of this new life.

Unbelief leads to disobedience, and both are sins against God. Those who know to do good and do not do it, to them it is sin. God cannot because of His holiness allow sin in His presence. God requires obedience on behalf of those who enter into this covenant with Him through Jesus Christ. This obedience is required if that person wants to remain in covenant fellowship with God. Christians who practice sinning have a light view of God's holiness and justice. They cannot live how they want to live, outside of God's Word, and expect to remain in fellowship with God. A sinning Christian is one who has forgotten the Lord his God.

God allows the believer to retain the sin nature, yet it is not to be used as an excuse to sin, to disobey God, because the believer puts his trust in the power of the Spirit of God to keep him from sinning by obeying the written Word of God. The Spirit will help the believer live out the Word of God that is in him, hidden in his heart. This is why faithful attendance at a Bible believing/preaching/teaching church, prayer, Bible study (personal and group), and daily quiet time alone with God and His Word are so vital to a life of endurance after you first believe. They are vital to completion of this walk by faith and to receiving the abundant life Christ came to give. When a person enters the covenant, when he first believes, he is a babe in Christ. He does not know how to live the Christian life. He must be taught by God now that he has become a child of God. His heavenly Father must train him in the way he ought to go so that as he grows old (matures in Christ) and as his faith increases he will not depart from it. The Father teaches His children by His Spirit through His Word from the mouth of the preacher, teacher, and evangelist. It is not by might, nor by power, but by God's Spirit that a believer will do what "thus says the Lord." The child of God must be taught God's truths, God's Word. And once he has been taught, he must obey it. The *Word* of righteousness produces *works* of righteousness when the child obeys it. To pursue righteousness as it is laid out before him in the Bible is to pursue the salvation of the Lord (to work out his salvation). The child of God must practice what he learns and knows from God's Word in order to grow. *God knows if you are His. The question is, "Do you know whether you belong to God?"*

Many are called but few are chosen. God called out the children of Israel (the nation of Israel) from among all the nations of the earth for the purpose of worshipping and serving Him. God wanted to show the idol worshipping nations the true and living God through the nation He called and separated unto Himself. God wants to show Himself to a lost and unbelieving world today through those who believe in His Son Jesus Christ. The purpose of the blood covenant with God through His Son Jesus is to bring life and peace to all mankind—to all nations. The covenant calls for reverence from all who enter in. God wants His name to be honored among His children. Hear God in Malachi 1:6: "A son honors his father, and a servant his master. If then I am the Father, where is My honor? And if I am a Master, where is My reverence?" God has concern for His holy name among those who are His.

The nation of Israel entered into a covenant agreement with God on Mt. Sinai to do what God commanded them to do and to live according to His ways, His instructions, and all that He told Moses. However, they all did not keep the covenant. As a result, they all did not enter the Promised Land, the land flowing with milk and honey. Many were called out of Egypt but only a few were chosen to enter that good land. Who did God choose? He chose those who remained loyal to Him (Numbers 14:20-30). Joshua and Caleb were the only two from the generation of those who were twenty years or older and were counted in the census when they came out of Egypt to inherit the promise. God chose Joshua and Caleb before the forty-year journey in the wilderness began because they believed the words God spoke concerning the land and the inhabitants. They followed the Lord their God completely; they gave a good report to Moses and the people. It was their confession of faith. They believed in their hearts that God would do what He had spoken. They believed that God's Word was truth and would not return to Him void. They trusted God's Word. Joshua and Caleb believed God when He said they would enter the Promised Land. How do we know? The Word of God tells us that they kept the covenant for forty years. Their fear (reverence) of God led to their faithfulness for forty years. They endured in obedience until the end. The other ten spies returned and gave a report on the people in the land of Canaan that caused the children of Israel to rebel. They spread discouraging reports about the land. The Word of God found no place in the unbelieving hearts of the ten. They were struck dead by a plague before the Lord.

All we have today is God's Word. Christians have nothing else on which to stand except God's Word. God asks us to trust His Word—that He will uphold and perform His Word. Those who trust God's Word show great faith, and their faith will be rewarded. We cannot see God with our natural eyes except in His creation. But we have His Word in order that we might see Him with our spiritual eyes. Do we believe God's Word? Do we trust God's Word? Do we live by God's Word? If we do then we believe that God is. We trust His Son is who He says He is and we live as Jesus lived, by every Word that proceeds from the mouth of God. We believe and trust in the Word from a God who is invisible to the natural eye. Now that is some kind of faith. But you see, this Word is not just any old word. It is the Word written by inspiration of God. Second Timothy 3:16 says, "All Scripture is given by inspiration of God." God's Word gives life to all who will believe it (1 Peter 1:23). God's Word is truth and the truth never changes.

Jesus came to earth on the Word of God. The angel Gabriel told Mary that the Holy Spirit would come upon her and the power of the Highest would overshadow her and that her son would be called the Son of God. Jesus died on the cross on the Word of God (Isaiah 53:12), and He rose from the grave on the Word of God (Matthew 28). How powerful is this Word of God! Jesus believed everything the Father told Him. He believed every word spoken from the mouth of God. We must learn and understand what we have in the Word of God's power. It is God's Word hidden inside the believer's heart that the Holy Spirit empowers as a life-changing force in his life. To believe on the name of the Lord Jesus Christ is to be "God dependent" every day of our lives. This dependency requires a lifetime commitment to God—His ways and His Word—through His Son. Jesus said, "If you love Me, obey my commandments." That love is a commitment to Him and His teachings. Jesus also said, "He who has My commandments and keeps them, it is he who loves Me. And he who loves Me will be loved by My Father, and I will love him and manifest Myself to him" (John 14:21). Did you notice that you must have Jesus' commandments (God's Word in your heart) and keep them, and then you will know that you love Jesus? Both Jesus and the Father will love the believer; they will commit themselves to him. Jesus is able to save to the uttermost all who come to God through Him.

God seals a person today as His own with His Spirit when he repents and believes the good report that Jesus Christ died for His sins (see 2 Corinthians 1:22 and Ephesians 4:30). When a person believes the Good News (the good report about Jesus), that person believes God, for it is God who has given witness that Jesus is His Son. God is witness that all the Bible says about Jesus is true.

"If we receive the witness of men, the witness of God is greater; for this is the witness of God which He has testified of His Son. He who believes in the Son of God has the witness in himself; he who does not believe God has made Him a liar, because he has not believed the testimony that God has given of His Son. And this is the testimony: that God has given us eternal life, and this life is in His Son. He who has the Son has life; he who does not have the Son of God does not have life." John wrote these things in 1 John 5 to those who believe in Jesus. Why? So that they may know that they have eternal life, and that they may continue to believe in the name of the Son of God. **The one who believes is the one who confesses Jesus as the Christ with his mouth and expresses his faith in Him and allegiance to Him by obedience to God's Word.** Out of the abundance of the heart the mouth speaks. You cannot confess Jesus as the Christ unless it is revealed to you from heaven through the work of the Holy Spirit (see 1 John 4:2-3). When Peter confessed that Jesus was the Christ, the Son of the living God, Jesus told Peter that he was blessed because His Father in heaven had revealed this to him (Matthew 16:13-17). And you cannot live a life of obedience without the Holy Spirit helping you. The Holy Spirit helps those today who are true believers to endure until the end. This race is not to the swift nor to the strong, but to those who endure until the end—until the end of their faith—which is the salvation of their soul.

Many are called to salvation today. But as the Israelites resisted Moses and did not obey God or keep the covenant, so do many professing Christians today resist God's Word. Why did the Israelites resist? Because they did not believe. Why do many professing Christians resist God's Word today? Because they do not believe. True faith changes the believer's conduct (how he lives). The purpose of obedience is to show that he belongs to God. A true Christian cannot believe in Jesus Christ and ignore the Word of God. If a man says he believes in Jesus, then he must (not optional) believe what the Bible says. Jesus is the Word who became flesh and dwelt among mankind. Jesus is the truth. The Word of God is truth. The Holy Spirit, given to all who believe, leads believers into all truth. Obedience is how God separates those who are His from those who are children of the devil. God calls the believer to live a holy (standing apart from sin and evil) and godly (faithful and devoted) life separated from the world. God calls the believer to total commitment and faithfulness to His Word. **God calls the believer to obey Him.** The true Christian's obedience will come from what God is doing in them as they are changed from glory to glory.

If a man or woman is a true child of God, if their lives are hidden in Christ, then God will see to it that none are lost. Not like Judas, the son of perdition. Jesus Christ will lose none that have been given to Him by the Father. Without Jesus we can do nothing that the Word of God tells us to do. If a professing Christian is not obeying God's Word, living a life of faith, obedience, and commitment unto God, then he must ask himself, "Am I really saved? Does Christ live in me? Am I really trusting in Christ? Am I really a true believer? Am I really following Christ? Am I on the road to salvation?" Why must he ask himself these questions? Because the Lord chastens (corrects by punishment or discipline with love) those He loves (His children). Why does God chasten His own children? Because of His holy name. It is for His holy name's sake, which believers profane among unbelievers when they sin against God. God will sanctify His great name which is profaned among the unbelievers, which the believers profane in their midst. The unbelievers shall know that God is the Lord when He is hallowed (honored) in His own children before the unbelievers' eyes.

God has made Himself personally responsible for seeing to it that everyone who belongs to Him makes it to the place Jesus has prepared for them in heaven. God loves everyone (John 3:16). But those "in" His love (His protective custody) are those who believe. They are the ones who are kept by the power of God through faith for salvation, ready to be revealed in the last time. Those professing Christians who are not disciplined by God (brought in line with His Word) are not His. This is something to think about if a person is living in sin (not living according to what the Bible teaches; disobeying God) and God has not brought the hand of correction upon him.

Psalm 37:3 reads, "Trust in the Lord and do good; dwell in the land and feed on His faithfulness." Before you can dwell in the land and feed on God's faithfulness, you must trust in the Lord and do good. You can only do good in Christ. "Delight yourself also in the Lord, and He shall give you the desires of your heart" (Psalm 37:4). The desire for the things of God will come only from God. The only way a man or woman can have the desire to live for Christ, to follow Him, and to want to do what is right and pleasing unto God, is if they have the Spirit of God dwelling inside their hearts. The Spirit of God leads them into all truth. The Spirit of God brings conviction when they sin against God. The Spirit of God makes a way of escape from temptation. The Spirit of God empowers them and helps them live the kind of life that God wants them to live. The Spirit of God is given as the guarantee of eternal inheritance to all who trust Jesus for salvation. The Spirit of God is the confirmation that they belong to God. "Then I will sprinkle clean water on you, and you shall be clean; I will cleanse you from all your filthiness and from all your idols. I will give you a new heart and put a new spirit within you; I will take the heart of stone out of your flesh and give you a heart of flesh. I will put My Spirit within you and cause you to walk in My statutes, and you will keep My judgments and do them" (Ezekiel 36:25-27).

You can be sure of this: "God has set apart the godly for Himself" (Psalm 4:3). The steps of the godly are directed by the Lord. He delights in every detail of their lives. Though they stumble, they will not fall, for the Lord holds them by the hand. The godly fill their heart with God's law, so they will never slip from His path. The godly hide God's Word in their heart so they will not sin against Him (Psalm 37:31). Note that the words *fill* and *hide* are actions the believer must take. These actions are done out of a heart of love. Love is an action word.

If you have not figured it out by now, you must understand that the promise of salvation from God is unconditional. However, God places demands on those who will receive this salvation. *God commands obedience to His Word from all who believe.* Paul tells us in Romans 2:7 that if we persist in doing what is good, seeking after the glory and honor and immortality that God offers, He will give us eternal life. In doing these things a Christian is storing up treasures in heaven. Hear King Solomon's prayer from 1 Kings 8:23 (NLT), "You keep your promises (**covenant**) and show unfailing love (**mercy**) to all who obey You and are eager to do Your will."

You can do nothing to earn or get this free gift of salvation. Jesus will save all who come to Him in faith. By your commitment to obedience, you show that you have been saved. All who submit to Jesus in obedience and as a humble servant, all who die to self, and all who pick up their cross daily and follow Him are true Christians.

Obedience is as simple as this: God says that all have sinned and fall short of His glory. Have we reached a state of perfection here on earth? Have we become like Christ (without sin) because we are Christians? No, we have not. Therefore, out of obedience, which is in keeping with what the Word of God teaches, we confess that we have sinned against God. We admit each day that we fall short of His glory. We admit that we have not kept His commandments; we have not fully obeyed His Word. David said, "For I acknowledge my transgression, and my sin is always before me. Against You, You only, have I sinned, and done this evil in your sight" (Psalm 51:3-4). So too should this be the prayer of the child of God. In word, thought, and deed we sin against God. God is a merciful and forgiving God, and He forgives our sins. He forgives us as often as there is confession and true repentance. There is true repentance when a person stops willfully committing the same sin over and over and over again, day after day after day, week after week after week. If we confess our sins, God is faithful and just to forgive us and to cleanse us from all unrighteousness (every wrong). Jesus said the sin that will not be forgiven men is blasphemy against the Holy Spirit (Matthew 12:31). As often as we confess our sins, as often as we obey God's Word, we are working out—not working for—our own salvation. Confessed sins are forgiven through the sacrifice of God's Son, the perfect Son who died on the cross.

God knows that we are weak, but He is strong. God shows Himself strong on behalf of those whose hearts are loyal to Him. God knows we cannot make the journey on our own. That is why He will never leave nor forsake His own. That is why He grants new mercies each day. For if God were to execute justice for our sins, who would live? The Lord's eyes and His heart will always be with His people.

He has consecrated (set apart) their temple (their body) so that His name will be honored there forever. The Son and the Father have made the believer's temple their dwelling place through the Spirit of God.

Some people know all the facts about Jesus' life as recorded in the Bible. They have read the Bible from Genesis to Revelation and yet they still reject Him. Mere knowledge of God's law (mental affirmation that what is written in the Bible is truth) does not bring God's approval. Head knowledge that Jesus is able to save and that He is the Savior of the world does not bring salvation. If those who know about Jesus will move from facts to faith, Jesus will save them. There must be a surrender of the rebellious heart by all who want eternal life. This surrender leads to a personal and intimate relationship with God. How will a man know if he knows Jesus (knows him personally, with his heart and not just his head)? In 1 John 2:3-6 (NLT) we read, "And how can we be sure we belong to Him [know Him]? By obeying His commandments."

If someone says "I belong to God (know God)" but does not obey His commandments, that person is a liar and does not live in the truth. But those who obey God's Word really do love Him. That is the way to know whether or not we live in Him. Those who say they live in God should live their lives as Christ did. In order for a believer to become like Christ (model His character and His lifestyle), he has to know Him. The way to know Him is through obedience to the Word of God. Those who obey God's Word will be declared right in God's sight. Without faith it is impossible to please God. Faith comes by hearing and hearing by the Word of God. To hear is to obey. Faith comes by obedience, and obedience comes by the Word of God.

Many attempt to portray their Christian faith through visible objects or conversation. They wear a cross around their neck. They wear T-shirts with words of faith written on them. They display symbols of faith on and inside their automobiles. They read books written by well-known authors who are teachers and ministers of God's Word. They quote the Scriptures. They often say how blessed they are by God because by worldly standards they have it all—good job, fine home, and drive the latest cars (American and foreign). They have a lot of this world's possessions, but they dishonor God by not keeping His Word.

Satan also knows the Scriptures (see Matthew 4). The children of the devil wear a cross around their necks, they wear the same kind of T-shirts, they read the same books written by Christians, they own the largest percentage of worldly possessions, and some even read the Bible and quote the Scriptures.

Wherein then does the difference lie between the children of God and the children of the devil? **The children of God live according to the instruction manual given to them by their heavenly Father. They live according to what the Bible teaches, not adding to it or taking away from it.** First John 3:10 tells us, "In this the children of God and the children of the devil are manifest: Whoever does not practice righteousness is not of God, nor is he who does not love his brother." God leads His children in the path of righteousness for His name's sake.

God is Creator of us all; He is the God of all flesh. But the unbelievers have as their god (master) the ruler of this world, Satan (the prince of darkness, the evil one). God is in control of their lives, but He is not for them but rather against them. He is not present in them nor is He with them. The Lord is God, but He is not their God (on an intimate and personal level), and He will not become their Father and they will not become His children until they come to Him through faith in Jesus. He will not dwell in an unclean temple. Read what Jesus said in John 14:23 as to where the Father and He will dwell.

Many confuse God's love with His blessings. God is kind to the unthankful and the evil for He is a merciful God. The Bible tells us that everyone benefits from the rain that falls and the sun that God allows to shine upon the earth. That is unconditional love for all humanity. The unbelievers, whom all Christians were at one time, receive God's mercy not His spiritual blessings. Spiritual blessings come from the Holy Spirit. As an example, God promises to forgive our sins as we forgive those who trespass against us. The unbeliever has not repented of nor confessed (acknowledged) his own sins against God. He has not forgiven anyone of their sins who has trespassed against him in the name of the One who died for his sins. Therefore, how can he receive God's blessing of forgiveness for his sins? Those who receive the spiritual blessings are those who walk by faith. Those who are blessed are those whose souls are right with God. Blessed is the condition of their souls as a result of being righteous because the blood of Christ covers them. The blood of Christ does not cover unbelievers, the children of the devil.

A sinning Christian conforms to the world and suppresses his nature given to him by God as a child of God. He obeys the flesh rather than the Spirit of God. He goes backward instead of progressing forward in his new life. He does not press toward the goal for the prize of his high calling. Jesus taught concerning building on a solid foundation in Matthew 7:21-27 when He said, "Not all people who sound religious are really godly. They may refer to Me as 'Lord,' but they still won't enter the kingdom of heaven. The decisive issue is whether they obey my Father in heaven. On judgment day many will tell me, 'Lord, Lord, we prophesied in your name and cast out demons in your name and performed many miracles in your name.' But I will reply, 'I never knew you. Go away.'" The one who professes to be a Christian yet sins against God must know whether or not he is building on a solid foundation.

Sin whispers to the wicked, deep within their hearts. They have no fear of God to restrain them. The godly fear God, and when sin whispers they take that thought captive and subject it unto the obedience of Christ in the power of the Spirit within their heart. They are transformed because their minds have been renewed by the power of Jesus Christ. They are tempted with the thought of disobedience/rebellion, yet they do not sin by acting or carrying out (yielding to) the thought. The godly no longer think like the world thinks. They no longer live like the world lives. The godly no longer follow the world and its wicked ways. They follow Jesus and His righteous ways. The godly no longer serve Satan. They no longer have a habit of sinning against God but rather serve the true and living God.

Can a man wallow in mud and wash/cleanse himself at the same time? No. And neither can a true believer practice sinning (willfully) against God and follow Jesus at the same time. He has to get out of the mud, the filth, in order to be cleansed. He, like the prodigal son, has to come to his senses and see his true condition as the Spirit of God is showing him. Sin stinks; it is an ugly sight to behold, and God cannot look upon it or allow the smell of it to enter His nostrils. When a man comes to Jesus for salvation, his heart must be turned toward Jesus. He must repent (change the way he thinks about sin). His heart must be broken from sin in order for him to enter into life. He must turn from sin to God. **In order to go up (to heaven), he must give up his rebellion against God. He must stop disobeying God by living in sin.**

The best expression of faith (belief) in Christ is obedience to the Word of God. The best expression of trust in Christ is obedience to His teachings (the Scriptures). Continued obedience is proof of a believer's love for Jesus. Through obedience a believer remains in Jesus' love. It is by grace through faith that he is saved. God's grace is His Son who died on the cross to set captives free. All mankind were slaves to sin. God's grace comes from the words of life that Jesus spoke. All who receive and believe them in their heart will live forever. All who confess with their mouth the Lord Jesus and believe in their heart that God raised Him from the dead will be saved. A man's salvation is by nothing that he can contribute to his own doing. The flesh profits nothing. It is the gift of God. Not of works lest anyone should boast.

Faith generates the kind of behavior that pleases God. This kind of God-pleasing faith will only come from the work the Holy Spirit is doing in the life of a true believer. He will not know what pleases God unless he knows the Scriptures. Willful ignorance of the Scriptures (the Word of God) is inexcusable for a Christian. This walk by faith is one day at a time, with the Holy Spirit leading the believer and the Word of God as his compass to guide him home to eternal life with Christ. If he stops believing, stops following Christ, stops following the Word of God, and if he goes his own way, then how will he get to heaven? How will he know the way? If he is not following Christ, then he is following Satan, the devil. God has a place of eternal fire (hell) prepared for the devil and his angels and all who follow him (his children) while on earth and die in their sins.

If we truly believe what the Bible says, we can take the Word of God written in John 6:68-69 and lay aside (put to rest) the teachings and doctrines of all other men, those who teach any other way to heaven. Jesus said that He is the way (the way to God, the way to heaven). Why? Because He alone has the words of eternal life (see also John 3:13-16). Jesus is the Word of life (1 John 1:1).

All roads and all religious beliefs do not lead to heaven, the throne of almighty God. All roads, except the one paved with the blood of Jesus Christ, lead to eternal ruin and ever-lasting destruction. A man's wealth, poverty, nor his religion will be the determining factor as to where he will end up in eternity. The determining factor will be whether or not he belonged to God. How can a man belong to God? By having faith in Jesus Christ. All religious doctrines that exclude Jesus Christ, the Son of the true and living God, as Lord and Savior of the world will not lead a man to heaven but to eternal separation from God if he continues in that belief.

The B.I.B.L.E—Believe It Before Leaving Earth

Jesus is coming back. The day of His return draws nearer each time a second, a minute, an hour, a day, a month, and a year passes by. If you are a professing Christian and you know after having read this message that you do not live according to how the Bible says you ought to live, then don't wait another second in getting your life right with God. Do not harden your heart to the truth. Let the truth set you free. Today is the day of your salvation. Repent and believe so that you may go with Jesus when He comes back for those who are His.

God tells those whose faith is in His Son Jesus Christ to obey His Word, to keep His commandments. Why? Because He is God and by obeying Him, He will always be their God and they His people. (See Jeremiah 7:23.) The voice from the cloud spoke to Peter and the two brothers, James and John, on the mountain when they witnessed Jesus' transfiguration and told them, "This is my beloved Son, and I am fully pleased with him. Listen to him" (Matthew 17:1-6 NLT).

I want to remind every believer reading this message about the terms of the covenant with God. This is what the Lord says: Cursed is anyone who does not obey the terms of this covenant. If you obey God and do whatever He commands you, then you will be His people and He will be your God. This message from God is clear: "Obey Me" (Jeremiah 11:7). If you want to live forever with God in heaven, you must obey His Word. You must live how He commands you to live while here on this earth. God will bring forth a new earth, and only those who are members of His family (the body of Christ) from this earth will inherit the new earth. Why will God bring forth a new earth? See Isaiah 24:5-6: "The earth is also defiled under its inhabitants, because they have transgressed the laws, changed the ordinance, broken the everlasting covenant. Therefore the curse has devoured the earth, and those who dwell in it are desolate. Therefore the inhabitants of the earth are burned, and few men are left."

If a man will not (notice I did not say *cannot* but *will not*) obey God on this earth that is passing away, God knows he will not obey Him on the earth that will last forever (see Isaiah 65:17; 66:22; Revelation 21:1-3). Obedience to the Word of God down here is proof that his heart has been changed. A person with an uncircumcised heart will not enter heaven.

That which is written in the Bible is trustworthy and true. The Word gives life to all (people of every nation and every tongue) who will believe. Why? Because in the beginning was the Word, and the Word was with God, and the Word was God. Jesus is the Word that became flesh and dwelt among us. If you believe the written Word of God, then you believe in Jesus Christ.

In closing, I want to leave you with this final thought to ponder: A true Christian is one who has received the Spirit of the living God, one who has the life of Christ in him. Christ's life will flow through the Christian's heart, mind and will each day. He can live as Jesus commands him to live with the Spirit's help, wisdom, power, and strength. The Holy Spirit of God will guide and lead him into all righteousness. A Christian hypocrite is one whose message about salvation does not line up with his own life. He says with his mouth, "I'm a Christian," but his actions, the life he lives, carries a different message. *What message is your life sending to the world?*

Heavenly Father, I pray that as those who believe have received Christ Jesus as their Lord, help them and teach them to walk in Him, letting their roots grow down into Him and drawing up nourishment from Him so they will grow in faith, abounding in it with thanksgiving. Amen.

QUESTIONS TO PONDER

The following list of questions, though not exhaustive or all-inclusive, is for you to use to see whether you are in the Christian faith, walking according to the gospel that you profess. Conduct an examination of your own life and see if it is a life of belief and obedience, a life of faith. Examine yourself to see if your faith is really genuine. You should look for an increased awareness of Christ's presence and power in your life.

1. Have I truly repented (a moral U-turn from sin to God)? Have I left the world behind and am I now committed to God? (Luke 3:8-9; Romans 2:7-8)
2. Who is it that I am serving, Christ or man? Look at your priorities in life and you will discover the answer. If the things of God and His kingdom business are your highest priority, then it is Christ whom you serve. (Matthew 6:24, 33)
3. Am I a member of a Bible-believing/teaching/ preaching church where I am being instructed in the truth and using the gifts/talents/abilities that God has given me? (1 Corinthians 12-14; 1 Thessalonians 5:14)
4. Why do I go to church and is my presence there making a difference in my own life and in the lives of others in the family of God? (Luke 6:46-49; 1 Corinthians 13:1-7)
5. How often do I attend church services (Bible study/ Sunday school/worship service)? (Exodus 20:8; Romans 10:17)

6. Do I have faith in God as evidenced by application of His Word in my life each day (James 1:22-25; 1 Thessalonians 1:5)? How often do I apply the truth from the Bible in my life (James 4:17; Isaiah 42:23)? How much of God's Word is hidden in my heart (Psalm 119:11)?

7. How much time do I devote to prayer? (1 Thessalonians 5:17)

8. How much time do I devote to reading/studying/meditating on God's Word? (Joshua 1:8; 2 Timothy 2:15)

9. How much time do I spend with other Christian sisters and brothers? (Hebrews 10:24-25; Psalm 119:63) How much time do I spend with the world, doing things that do not glorify God? (James 4:4)

10. Have I received power from God? Am I being used by God to build up His kingdom? When did I last tell someone the good news of salvation? How often do I witness (share the gospel/my testimony) to others? (Acts 1:8; Colossians 1:6)

11. What kind of things do I think about the most—heavenly (eternal) or earthly (temporary)? Where is my treasure (my heart)? (Colossians 3:1-2; Matthew 6:21)

12. Am I engaged in activities/relationships that I know are wrong and displeasing to God? (Galatians 5:19-21; Colossians 3:5-9)

13. Do I understand the impact that unconfessed sins to God have on my relationship with God? Am I confessing my sins to God each day? (Psalm 66:18; Matthew 6:12; 1 John 1:9-10)

14. Does the life I live draw people to Christ or turn them away? (Matthew 5:14; 2 Corinthians 4:4; Colossians 3:12-17)

15. Am I living as if I really believe Jesus Christ is coming back again while not knowing the day or the hour? (Matthew 24:36-44; 1 Thessalonians 5:1-10; James 5:7-12)

CHAPTER 7

GOD – THE SOVEREIGN LORD OF HEAVEN AND EARTH

What should true Christians know and understand about the God they serve? They should know and understand that He is the Lord, the God of all flesh.

The Most High God gave King Nebuchadnezzar (a pagan ruler who worshipped other gods) a kingdom and majesty, glory and honor. And because of the glory that God gave him, all peoples, nations, and languages trembled and feared before him. But when Nebuchadnezzar's heart was lifted up, and his spirit was hardened in pride, he was deposed from his kingly throne, and they took his glory from him. He was driven from the sons of men, his heart was made like the beasts, and his dwelling was with the wild donkeys. They fed him with grass like oxen, and his body was wet with the dew of heaven, till he knew that the Most High God rules in the kingdom of men, and appoints over it whomever He chooses. (Daniel 5:18-21) Hear now the words uttered from the mouth of King Nebuchadnezzar of Babylon after God humbled him, brought him down low. "His rule is everlasting and His kingdom is eternal. All the people of the earth are nothing compared to Him. He has the power to do as He pleases among the angels of heaven and with those who live on earth. No one can stop Him or challenge Him saying, 'What do you mean by doing these things?'" (Daniel 4:34-35 NLT). God knows how to humble every prideful and rebellious heart so that the one who possesses it will recognize His sovereign rule in their life. **One day every (no one is excluded) knee will bow and every tongue confess that Jesus Christ is Lord (Philippians 2:10-11).**

Moses said to God, "Indeed when I come to the children of Israel and say to them, The God of your fathers has sent me to you, and they say to me, 'What is His name?' what shall I say to them?" And God said to Moses, "**I AM WHO I AM.**" And He said, "Thus you shall say to the children of Israel, "I AM has sent me to you" (Exodus 3:13-14). Who is God, except the Lord!

I AM the First and **I AM** the Last. **I AM** the Lord, the true and living God, and besides Me there is no other.

I AM the God who spoke and said, "Let there be," and it was so...just as **I** commanded it.

I AM the God who is Creator and Possessor of heaven and earth. All things are Mine.

I AM your Creator. **I AM** the God who has the power to give life and to take it away.

I AM the God who laid the foundations of the earth and who determined its measurements.

I AM the God who stretched out the heavens and set the boundaries for the oceans and the seas.

I AM the God who has commanded the morning since your days began and caused the dawn to know its place.

I AM the God who can do everything and no purpose of Mine can be withheld from Me.

I AM the God whose Word once spoken shall not return unto Me void but it shall accomplish what **I** please and it shall prosper in the thing for which **I** sent it.

I AM the God whose throne is heaven and earth My footstool.

I AM the God whom no one can contend with.

I AM the God who is the Light that shines in darkness.

I AM the Lord, the God of all flesh. Is there anything too hard for Me?

I AM the God who preserves both man and beast.

I AM the God who has the power to take a man's life and cast his soul into hell.

I AM the God who alone knows the number of your days and your end from your beginning.

I AM the God who is love. **I** send rain on the just and the unjust and **I** make the sun rise on the evil and the good.

I AM the God who gives wisdom to the wise and knowledge to those who have understanding.

I AM the God who knows all things…sees all things…hears all things. Nothing a man does escapes Me. There is nothing covered that will not be revealed, and hidden that will not be known.

I AM the God who rules in the kingdom of men and gives it to whomever **I** choose.

I AM the God who will keep him in perfect peace whose mind is stayed on Me. Because he trusts in Me.

I AM the God who knows your thoughts afar off.

I AM the God who chose David as My servant, a man after My own heart, to rule over My people Israel.

I AM the God who gave life to Sarah's dead womb that she might bring forth the promise.

I AM the God who answers before you call. **I AM** the God who hears while you are still speaking.

I AM the God who sent My Angel and shut the lions' mouths so that they would not harm my servant Daniel. **I AM** the only God who can deliver. **I AM** the Lord.

I AM the God who holds your breath in My hand and owns all your ways.

I AM the God of mercy and truth. **I AM** a just God.

I AM the Alpha and the Omega...the Beginning and the End. **I AM** the Lord who is and who was and who is to come, the Almighty.

I AM the Lord your God...the Holy One of Israel, your Savior.

I AM the God whose ways and thoughts are higher than your ways and thoughts.

I AM the God whom you seek and find when you search for Me with all your heart.

I AM the God who knew you before you were formed in your mother's womb. I know the plan that I have for you.

I AM your Father. **I AM** the One who named you...who called you to Myself.

I AM the Way, the Truth, and the Life.

I AM the God who is the Author and Finisher of your faith.

I AM the God they hated without a cause.

I AM the God who gave My back to those who whipped Me (thirty-nine stripes I received) and **I AM** the God who gave My cheek to the one who struck me and to those who plucked out My beard.

I AM the God who did not hide His face from shame and spitting.

I AM the God whose visage was marred more than any man.

I AM the God upon whose head a crown of thorns was placed.

I AM the God who after suffering all of this, still endured and walked the hill to Cavalry.

I AM the God they crucified and hung on a tree. **I AM** the God who was numbered with the transgressors and bore the sins of many.

I AM the God with all power in My hands…the God who died and rose again, and who conquered death that you might be set free…set free to serve Me.

I AM the God who laid down My life and took it up again. No man took My life from Me.

I AM the God who proclaimed, "O death, where is thy sting? O grave, where is thy victory?"

I AM WHO I AM. I AM all you need in this world. For in Me you have all things. **I AM** your exceedingly great reward.

I AM the God who suffers long, desiring that no man perish but all come to repentance.

In Christ I AM your God and you are My people…created to serve and worship Me for all eternity.

Printed in the United States
49566LVS00002B/256-279